Adorable Mini Animals to Crochet

Marie Clesse

Photography by Claire Payen

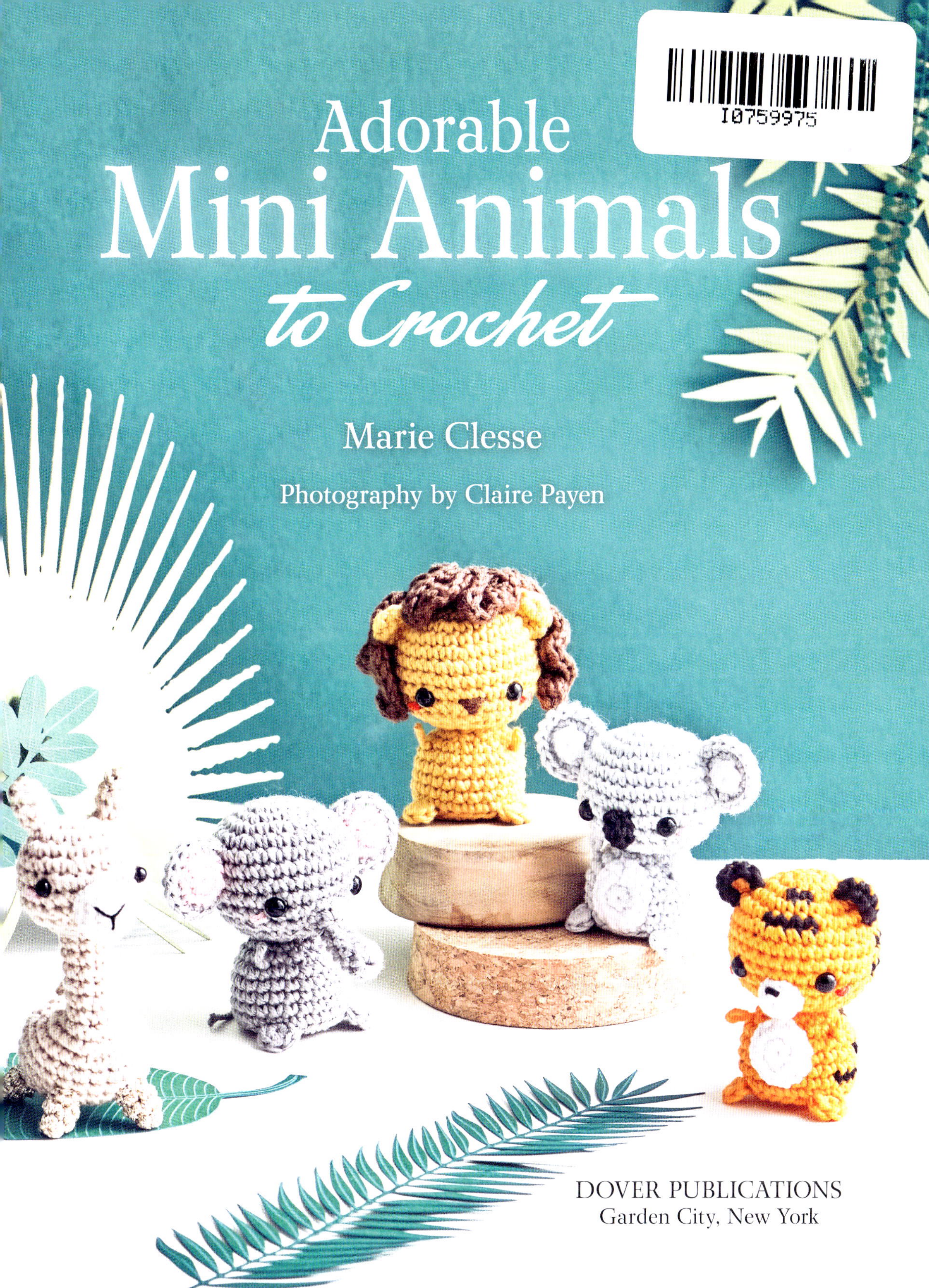

DOVER PUBLICATIONS
Garden City, New York

I would like to offer a big thanks to all the members of Mango Éditions who have invested in this fourth joint project, and in particular to Mélanie Jean, my editor. Mélanie, it is always a joyful pleasure to work with you. Thank you so much for that. I hope we will make many more beautiful projects together!

Thank you to DMC for again being a partner in my work, especially Charline Binckly, with whom it is always a pleasure to exchange ideas. I love working with this Happy Cotton.

Thank you to Delphine Thorner, a talented proofreader, with whom I feel lucky to collaborate.

Thank you to Claire Payen, photographer, for this journey, so rich with learning in the studio, and for this cover that I adore.

I repeat myself a little bit from one book to the next, but it is so important to say it... Thank you with all my heart to my family and my friends, all of you who form this solid little circle that is always enthusiastic and supportive. I am very lucky to be so well surrounded.

And finally, thank you with all my heart to you who read these acknowledgments and who will perhaps soon crochet your own mini animals.

Thank you for sharing my creative adventure and for making all this possible.

THE YARNS

The editor and the author thank DMC for the magnificent yarns that were used for the creation of the designs.

This Dover edition, first published in 2024, is a new English translation of *Adorables mini animaux* by Marie Clesse, with photography by Claire Payen, published by Mango, Paris, France, in 2020. The original French work has been translated into English by Janet Ross Snyder.

ISBN-13: 978-0-486-85385-7
ISBN-10: 0-486-85385-3

Publisher: Betina Cochran
Acquisitions Editor: Allyson D'Antonio
Managing Editorial Supervisor: Susan Rattiner
Cover Designer: Peter Donahue
Creative Manager: Marie Zaczkiewicz
Interior Designer: Jennifer Becker
Production: Pam Weston, Tammi McKenna, Ayse Yilmaz

Printed in China
85385301 2024
www.doverpublications.com

Introduction

If you have been following my work for a while, you may know that these mini animals are what I started with when I first offered *amigurumi* for sale, almost four years before the publication of this book. Soothed in my childhood by stories of my mother and her miniature dolls that lived in a matchbox, I have always nurtured a kind of adoration for all things tiny. When I wanted to create my first animal designs, it was obvious to me that they should be tiny and endearing, just like all those figurines that I loved collecting in my childhood.

Since then, I have created more than forty designs of mini animals, and I have crocheted hundreds that have joined you in the four corners of the world. So writing this book, and finally offering these patterns you have so often asked me for, has been a particular treat for me: a cherished connection to my beginnings.

Don't believe that this was simple! It was necessary to select the animals for this book, and leave some out because of lack of space, all while trying not to forget the ones you liked the most... I confess that I would have liked to fit them all into these pages! I hope that you will be happy with the result, and that you will have a lot of fun crocheting swarms of mini animals, whether to put together an adorable zoo for your children, or to keep them all for yourself!

You will understand why this book has a particular place in my heart, and I hope that it will find its way into yours as well.

Marie

Contents

Exotic Animals

pp. 30–38

Elephant and Tiger

pp. 32 and 35

Lion, Koala, and Alpaca

pp. 30, 31, and 37

Parakeet

p. 34

Unicorn

p. 39

Dinosaur

p. 40

Farm Animals

pp. 42–47

Duck, Ducklings, and Cat

pp. 42, 43, and 46

Forest Animals

pp. 48–54

Fox, Rabbit, and Fawn

pp. 48, 49, and 50

Fawn and Squirrel

pp. 50 and 52

Rabbit and Owl

pp. 49 and 53

Sea Creatures

pp. 55–63

Octopus and Whale, pp. 55 and 58

Octopus and Penguin, pp. 55 and 56

Shark, p. 60

Shark and Turtle. pp. 60 and 62

Materials

YARNS

The designs in this book have been crocheted with DMC Happy Cotton yarn, which I find perfect for *amigurumi*. You can easily find this yarn in stores and online shops.

For each design, you will find the yarn and thread colors used and the necessary quantities of each. However, feel free to use the yarn of your choice. If you choose another yarn, you must make sure to use a smaller crochet hook than the one recommended on the yarn ball. That way you can avoid having holes between the stitches and won't see the stuffing through the holes.

If you are a beginner, make sure to choose a yarn that is tightly spun. A yarn that splits can become very frustrating for a beginner (or even for a seasoned crocheter). In general, you are better off working with good quality yarns. They make the work much more pleasant.

Do not hesitate to try some of these patterns with a thicker cotton yarn, such as DMC Natura Just Cotton Medium, to be crocheted with a 3mm or 3.5mm hook, according to the suppleness desired. That will give you even larger animals that are 8cm high instead of 6cm, perfect for making little stuffed toys or cute decorations for a child's room.

HOOKS

This table shows the correspondence between metric crochet hook sizes, US sizes, and UK sizes.

Metric	US	US Steel	UK	UK Steel
2mm	0	4	14	2½
2.25mm	B-1	2	13	1½
2.5mm	B-1 or C-2	2 or 1	13 or 12	1½ or 1
4mm	G-6		8	

To crochet these miniatures, I have used a 2.25mm crochet hook, and I crochet tightly, so as to make them quite rigid. However, you can choose to crochet them with a 2.5mm crochet hook to produce a result that is a little more supple. Your animals will then be a little bigger as well. Nevertheless, I advise against using a larger crochet hook with this thickness of cotton, because the stitches would then be much more spaced out, and that would be very noticeable on such small designs.

I cannot stress enough how important it is to invest in a good quality crochet hook. For my part, I prefer ergonomic crochet hooks, even though I hold my crochet hook in a nonstandard way, like a knife. But others may prefer a simple steel or aluminum hook. Do not hesitate to test a crochet hook design before launching into the purchase of a complete set. A good crochet hook should slide easily between the stitches, and its point must not get caught on the threads, to avoid splitting them.

STUFFING

I use polyester stuffing, treated for dust mites. It is easy to buy online in 300g (10oz), 500g (1lb), or 1kg (2lb) bags. You can also find it in yarn shops, craft stores, or fabric stores, or in a pinch, you can reuse the stuffing from a pillow! It is difficult to indicate the quantity you will need for each design, because it all depends on whether you prefer to stuff lightly or firmly. However, a 300g (10oz) bag will likely be enough to make all the designs in this book.

To make some of these mini animals, I also use plastic pellets, 5mm in diameter. These little granules give a certain weight to the body and thus a better balance to the little figures. They are a good alternative to classic

stuffing, because they do not cause the body to bulge, and they make it possible for the base to remain flat.
If you don't want to use plastic pellets, I would advise you to use a stuffing that is not too fluffy, so as not to deform the body and to keep its base nice and flat.
If you use plastic pellets, it is important to use a small crochet hook so that the stitches are tight and the little pellets cannot escape.
The stuffing (polyester batting or pellets) must be dense enough to give shape to the project, but not so dense that it spreads out the stitches; if you stuff too densely, you will see the stuffing between each stitch, which is not pleasing and might even prove dangerous for young children.

Tip: I always wait several hours after having stuffed the head before sewing it onto the body. It is then easier to judge whether a little stuffing is missing somewhere, and to make adjustments so that the head is nicely round and harmonious.

SAFETY EYES

The size to be used is indicated for each design (between 4.5mm and 8mm [1/5in and ⅓in]). These plastic eyes are sold with a washer that is attached to the back on a notched stem; this guarantees that the eyes cannot be removed. They are rather difficult to find in small sizes. If you do not find them at your favorite local shop, I suggest that you look for them on the internet, where you will find a vast selection. You may also use black beads instead, or even embroider the eyes with black thread, which is recommended if your *amigurumi* are likely to be handled by children younger than three years of age.

OTHER MATERIALS

- Yarn needle and a finer needle for the Pearl Cotton threads.
- Pins to hold the pieces together while assembling them.
- Stitch markers. If you have none, you may instead use a small safety pin, a paper clip, or a small piece of thread passed through the stitch to mark it.
- Scissors.
- Flat pliers. They are very useful for stuffing the small crocheted parts, for adding a bit of stuffing to a precise location, and for pulling a needle through several thicknesses of wool and stuffing (and for saving your fingers).
- Optional: pipe cleaners (chenille stems) for the tails of certain animals, and a permanent felt marker to color the cheeks.

Techniques

The following explanations are given for someone who holds the crochet hook in the right hand. If you are left-handed, you will need to follow the explanations using a mirror image.

THE BASIC STITCHES

Chain stitch (ch): stitches in the air

1. Make a slip knot: insert the crochet hook in the loop of the knot, then, using the point of the hook, catch the yarn coming from the ball or skein and bring it back through the loop. This slip knot is the starting point, but it never counts as a stitch.

2. To make a chain stitch (ch), yarn over (pass the yarn from back to front, over the crochet hook) and bring this yarn through the loop of the hook.

3. Repeat the second step until you obtain the desired number of stitches. The loop on the crochet hook must never be counted.

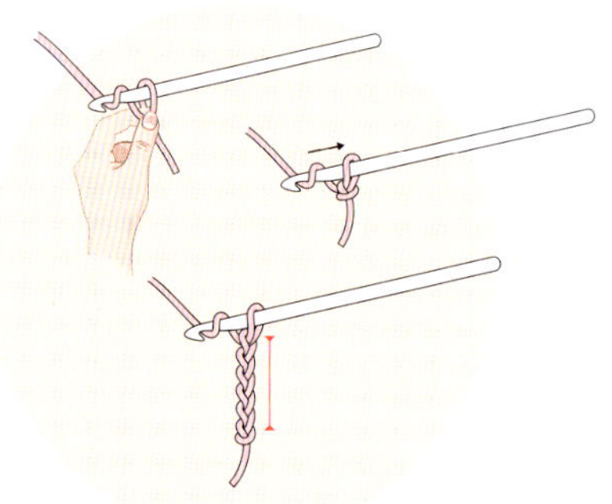

Slip stitch (sl st)

1. Insert the crochet hook in the stitch indicated.

2. Yarn over (yo) and bring the yarn through the stitch where the hook is and through the loop on the crochet hook. There should be one loop left on the crochet hook.

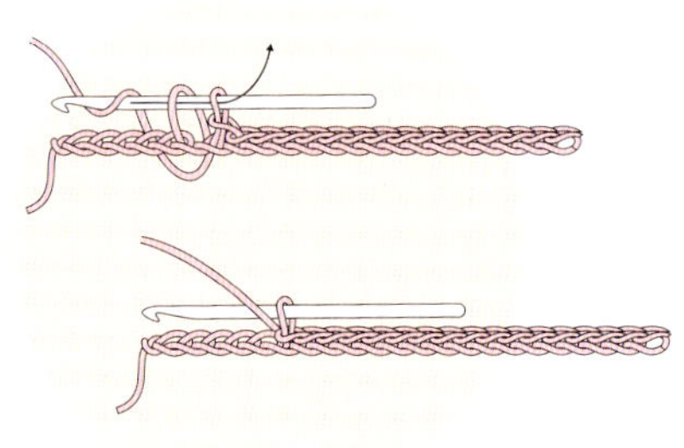

Single crochet (sc)

1. Insert the crochet hook into the stitch indicated.

2. Yarn over and bring the yarn through the stitch where your hook is. There should be two loops left on the hook.

3. Yarn over a second time and bring the yarn through the two loops. There should be one loop left on the crochet hook.

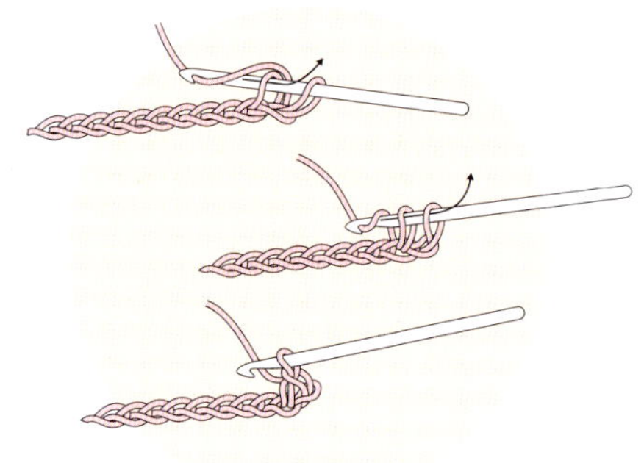

Half double crochet (hdc)

1. Yarn over, then insert the crochet hook into the stitch indicated.

2. Yarn over a second time and bring the yarn through the stitch where your hook is. There should be three loops on the crochet hook.

3. Yarn over one last time and bring the yarn through the three loops. There should be one loop left on the crochet hook.

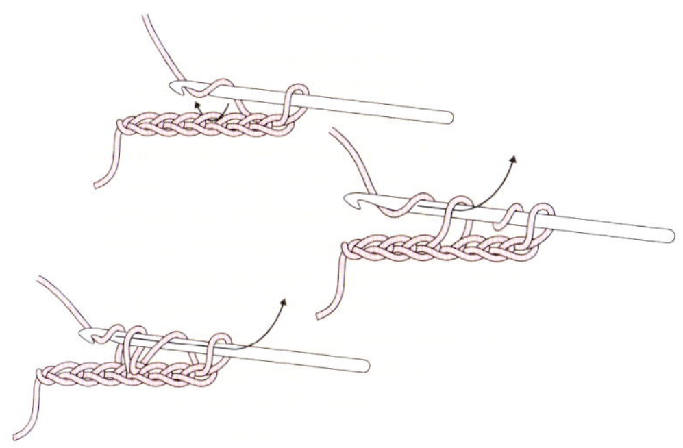

Double crochet (dc)

1. Yarn over, then insert the crochet hook into the stitch indicated.

2. Yarn over a second time and bring the yarn back through one loop. There should be three loops left on the crochet hook.

3. Yarn over a third time and bring the yarn back through two loops. There should be two loops on the crochet hook.

4. Yarn over one last time and bring the yarn back through the two loops. There should be one loop left on the crochet hook.

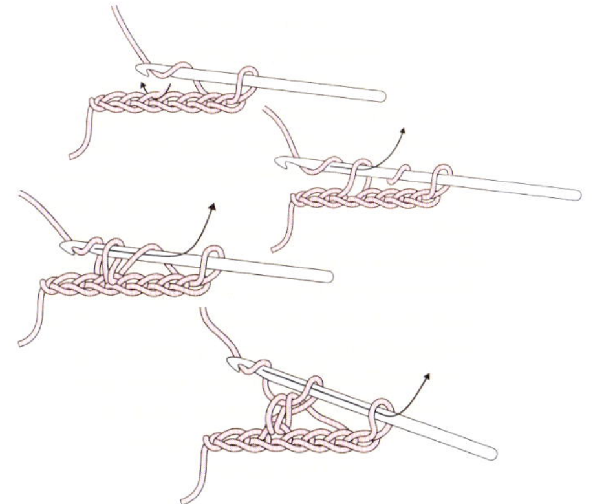

Treble crochet (tr)

1. Yarn over twice, then insert the crochet hook into the stitch indicated.

2. Yarn over a third time and bring the yarn back through the stitch where the crochet hook is. There should be four loops on the crochet hook.

3. Yarn over a fourth time and bring the yarn back through two loops. There should be three loops on the crochet hook.

4. Yarn over a fifth time and bring the yarn back through two loops. There should be two loops left on the crochet hook.

5. Yarn over one last time and bring the yarn back through the two loops. There should be one loop on the crochet hook.

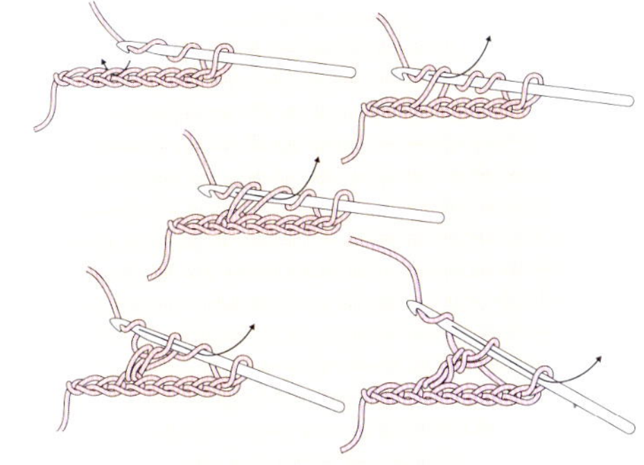

WHERE DO I INSERT THE CROCHET HOOK?

Unless otherwise indicated, always insert the hook from the front to the back.

In a chain

Insert the crochet hook into the upper loops of the chain. At the end of the chain, turn the work to the other side if you are crocheting in rows, or continue crocheting around the end of the chain to form an oval. In this case, continue crocheting on the chain, but this time in the lower loops.

In the stitches of a preceding row

The top of a crocheted stitch always has two small loops forming a horizontal V, no matter what type of stitch you are making. Unless you are instructed otherwise, always insert the crochet hook under both of these loops.

In the front loop only (FLO)

When this instruction is given, insert the crochet hook only in the front loop; that is, the loop of the V that is closest to you, on the front side of the work.

In the back loop only (BLO)

When this instruction is given, insert the crochet hook only in the back loop, that is, the loop of the V that is farthest away from you, on the back side of the work.

CROCHETING IN ROWS

Working in rows always starts with a chain that serves as a base. Crochet from right to left, turning the work (clockwise) at the end of each row. The last stitch crocheted thus becomes the first stitch of the next row. Working in rows makes it necessary to start with one or more chain stitches at the start of each row, depending on the height of the stitches that make up the row. (This will be indicated in the instructions for the designs concerned.)

CROCHETING IN THE ROUND

Working in the round (rnd) is the technique that is most often used to make *amigurumi*. It makes it possible to work continuously, without turning the work. Working in the round starts by making a magic circle (or a chain if you want to make an oval piece), and then you can work in a spiral or you can close each round with a slip stitch.

Simple magic circle

This technique makes it possible to tighten the first round so that there is no hole at the center of the work. Hold the end of the yarn between the thumb and index finger of your left hand. Wrap it around your index finger, making one turn. Hold the part of the yarn connected to the ball with the middle finger and the ring finger. Insert the crochet hook under the loop formed on the index finger (between the yarn and the underside of your finger) and bring back the yarn attached to the ball. Make a chain stitch. The center ring is ready. Starting from there, crochet the number of stitches indicated in the loop thus formed. All that is left to do is to pull the end of the yarn to tighten the circle. Secure this yarn, if necessary, by crocheting it into the stitches of the second round.

Crocheting in a spiral

This technique consists of crocheting continuously, without closing the rounds.
At the end of a round, simply continue crocheting in the next stitch, which is the first stitch of the round that you just finished.
It is important to use a stitch marker to keep your place in your work. Place this marker on the first stitch of each round. On the last stitch of the round, remove the marker, make the first stitch of the following round, and place the marker over it.

Crocheting in closed rounds

This technique consists of closing each round before moving on to the following one.
After making the last stitch of the round, make a slip stitch in the first stitch made at the start of the round. This stitch closes the round, and it is never counted in the stitch count of the round.
To start a new round, first make the number of chain stitches corresponding to the type of stitch that you are going to crochet on this round, to reach the correct height: one chain for single crochet, two for half-double crochet, three for double crochet, etc. When you work in closed rounds, this chain is not counted in the stitch count for the round. Next, make the first stitch of the new round in the first stitch of the preceding round (the same one in which you just made a slip stitch).
Even though it is easier to keep your place in the work by crocheting in this manner, I advise you to mark the first stitch of each round all the same.
I am often asked why I crochet certain parts in closed rounds in the designs. It is, in fact, more common to crochet amigurumi in a spiral. Crocheting in closed rounds has its advantages. First of all, it makes color changes clearer for a striped design. For certain pieces, it also makes it possible to have a result that is straighter or more level. However, if you are having difficulty with this technique, it is quite possible to crochet in a spiral instead.
Trick: It is easy to make the demarcation that is formed with the slip stitch to close each round almost invisible. All you have to do is tighten this stitch to the maximum while crocheting the rest normally!

INCREASES

An increase consists of simply making two stitches in the same stitch of the preceding round or row. The *amigurumi* or other crocheted objects are made essentially with single crochet. Also, when you see the abbreviation "inc," it means that you must make two single crochets in the same stitch.

It sometimes happens that you must increase another type of stitch. In this case, the instruction will be, for example, "two half double crochets in the same stitch." You may also be instructed to make "three single crochets in the same stitch." Follow the instructions exactly to obtain the expected results.

DECREASES

A decrease consists of crocheting two stitches together to obtain only one at that place. I mainly use the technique of invisible decreases. When you find the abbreviation "dec," it means that you must crochet two single crochets together. To do that, instead of inserting the crochet hook under both loops of the stitch, insert it in the front loop of the stitch, then immediately insert it in the front loop of the following stitch. Next make a single crochet. If you must make a decrease in a half double, follow the same method: yarn over as you would do for a normal half double, then insert the crochet hook in the front loop of the first stitch and immediately afterward in the front loop of the following stitch. Yarn over again, bring the yarn back through these two front loops. Then yarn over again and bring the yarn back through the three loops on the crochet hook.

To decrease the number of stitches in a round, it is sometimes necessary to flow the stitches together. This consists of making incomplete stitches (you do not make the last yarn over of these stitches), in order to flow them together when you make the final, common yarn over. For example, to flow two single stitches together, you must follow these steps:

- Insert the crochet hook as indicated in the following stitch, yarn over and bring back the yarn. At this point, there are two loops on the crochet hook.
- Instead of finishing this single stitch, insert the crochet hook in the following stitch, yarn over, and bring back the yarn. There are now three loops on the crochet hook.
- Do a last yarn over and bring back the yarn through the three loops on the crochet hook. Now there is only one loop on the hook. To flow together another type of stitch, always proceed in the same manner by following all the steps of the stitch in question, except for the last yarn over. After having made the number of incomplete stitches to flow together (there can be more than two of them), do a last yarn over and bring back the yarn through all the loops on the crochet hook.

COLOR CHANGES

It is important to do a color change at the place indicated in order to obtain the desired result. But to obtain a neat result, you must start at the previous stitch!

To do this, when you crochet the last stitch before the color change, follow these steps:

- Start the single crochet normally. Insert the crochet hook, yarn over, and pull the yarn toward the stitch. You now have two loops on the crochet hook.
- Change the color at that moment by doing a yarn over with the new color, and bring this yarn through the two loops on the hook. There is now one loop of the new color on the crochet hook.
- Next, continue to crochet with this new color. Make a knot on the back side of the work with the yarn of the old color and the starting yarn of the new color.

Sometimes you have to make repeated color changes. In this case, it is preferable not to cut the old color yarn, but to keep it attached so that you can start to crochet with it again in the next round.

RIGHT SIDE OR WRONG SIDE OF THE STITCHES?

It is sometimes difficult for beginners to figure out which is the right side or the wrong side of their work. If you are right-handed, when you insert the crochet hook from the front to the back (that is, from the outside to the inside as the piece begins to take its rounded shape), the right side of the work is toward you (that is, the outside as the piece begins to take shape).

For pieces crocheted in the round, it is easier to crochet if you keep the right side of the work to the outside. You can choose to keep the back side visible for aesthetic reasons, but that presents two difficulties. First, the back side of the work is more disorganized. The back side of the single stitches presents a succession of little horizontal features that form lines, and the stitches are more difficult to see and to count. The right side of the single stitches forms little Vs that are much easier to count. The major difficulty of the back side of the work is that it is more difficult to make invisible decreases there. Depending on the project that you are making, the decreases will be much more visible, and the finished product will be less attractive.
Train yourself to tell the front from the back with a few rounds of single crochet, and then observe the difference by testing other types of stitches!

FINISHING TECHNIQUES

Clean finishes are very important for an attractive result. Here is how to stop and close the various crocheted pieces.

Stopping the yarn invisibly

When you work in a spiral, without closing the rounds, you obtain a sort of stairstep—the edge is not clean. To improve this uneven edge, the instructions will ask you to finish with a slip stitch.
Cut the yarn to about 6in (15cm) and thread a needle with it. Skip over the following stitch and pass the needle under the next two back loops, going from the inside to the outside of the piece. Then pass the needle under the back loop of the slip stitch by inserting it toward the inside of the piece. Make a knot on the back side of the work, or keep the length of the yarn for sewing, according to the instructions given.
This technique reproduces the two loops of a stitch above the stitch that you skipped. That makes it possible to obtain a clean result without having to change the number of stitches.

Closing a piece

After making the last stitch, cut the yarn off at a length of about 8in (20cm). With a needle, pass the yarn under the front loop of the following stitch, from the inside toward the outside. Do the same with all the stitches of the last crocheted round (generally 5 or 6 stitches). Then pull the yarn to close the opening.
Pass this yarn through the central hole and bring it out the other side of the crocheted piece. Adjust the tension so that it is well closed, but not enough to crush the piece. Pass the yarn through the piece once or twice more to secure the closure. Cut the yarn off flush with the surface of the piece.

ASSEMBLY

Sewing two open pieces together, edge to edge (head and body, for example)

When the last rounds of the two pieces have the same number of stitches, simply pass the thread alternately through one stitch of the body (from the inside toward the outside) and then through a stitch of the head (from the outside to the inside). Make sure to verify the alignment of the head and the body after several stitches, and restart if necessary by shifting the first stitch. After making the last stitch, make several more stitches to secure the closure, and then cut the thread off flush with the surface of the piece.

Sewing one piece onto another

These seams are a little more complicated and are often the pet peeve of crocheters! You will improve with practice. Position the piece to be sewn at the desired place, and pin it there so it does not move. You must sew all the stitches of the last round to obtain a good-looking finish. Insert the needle under a thread of the closed piece, and then under both loops of the stitch of the last round, from the inside to the outside. Repeat this operation to sew all the stitches. Before making the last sewing stitches, add a little stuffing, if necessary. To finish, make several more stitches, and cut the yarn off flush with the surface.
When crocheting these mini animals, you will notice that I sew certain elements before stuffing the head or the body. In fact, I often prefer to knot the sewing yarn on the inside, rather than stopping it by making several more stitches.

Since the seams are small, like the animals, that ensures a more secure attachment.
For example, it would be difficult to have the front or back paws very tightly attached to the body without making a very tight knot on the back side. On the other hand, the pellet stuffing used for the body does not help hold seams the way polyester stuffing does (the stuffing used for the head), because the yarn does not get trapped on the inside by the pellets the way it does with the polyester stuffing. However, it is quite possible to sew all the elements of the head after having stuffed it, if you are more comfortable doing it that way.
For the body, if you find it difficult to figure out the position of the tummy or the tail, try it like this: lightly stuff the body with the polyester stuffing to give its shape; sew the necessary elements in place, being careful not to catch too much stuffing in the stitches; remove the extra stuffing (some will remain stuck to the sewing stitches, but this is not a problem); knot the yarn on the inside of the body; and finally, stuff the body with the plastic pellets.

EMBROIDERY

Several designs have instructions to embroider elements on the face (smile, eyebrows, etc.). If you know exactly where to place them, you can embroider before stuffing the piece and simply make a knot on the back side of the work. However, it is often difficult to evaluate the correct placement before stuffing. To embroider the elements after stuffing, take a long, fine needle and insert it between two stitches at the back of the piece, or in the stuffing through the opening of the piece, and bring it back out at the place where the embroidery should go. Embroider the elements, then bring the thread back out exactly where it went in at the back of the piece, or through the stuffing again. Make a knot with the two threads, then push the knot inside the piece to make it invisible. With a needle, if necessary, push the two ends inside and cut off any part that is still sticking out.

SOME ADVICE BEFORE STARTING

To produce smooth work, do not tighten the stitches too much. The crochet hook should be able to pass easily through the stitches, and you should always keep the same tension on your yarn. If you are a beginner, practice making the basic stitches before starting the first design. That will help you feel at ease with the various basic stitches and their abbreviations, and not be obliged to constantly refer to the *Techniques* section of the book.
Feel free to vary the size of the crochet hook depending on the way you crochet: If you crochet more loosely, you may benefit from using a smaller crochet hook. On the other hand, if you tend to crochet more tightly, you may want to choose a larger crochet hook.
Read the instructions for a design completely before beginning to make sure that you understand everything and that you have not overlooked important information.
The estimated time to make each animal has been provided as a rough guide but may vary according to your crocheting experience. The duration indicated includes the time I spend reading the instructions as I go and crocheting at a relaxed speed.
Attention! These mini animals are not appropriate for children younger than three years old. However, if you decide to make a design for very young children, I advise you to replace the safety eyes with embroidered eyes, and to use a small crochet hook, to prevent holes between the stitches that could allow stuffing to come out.

ABBREVIATIONS

BL = back loop
BLO = in the back loop only
ch = chain stitch(es)
dc = double crochet(s)
dec = invisible decrease
FL = front loop
FLO = in the front loop only
hdc = half double crochet(s)
inc = increase
rnd(s) = round(s)
row(s) = row(s)
sc = single crochet(s)
st = stitch(es)
sl st = slip stitch(es)
tr = treble crochet(s)
( ) x 6 = crochet items in the parentheses six times
(6 st) = number of stitches for each round

Basic Shapes

HEAD

Embroidered eyes: To replace the safety eyes with embroidered eyes, all you have to do is embroider two or three small vertical black lines, one row high, starting from the location indicated for each eye.

Cheeks: I use two techniques for these mini animals. Some cheeks have been drawn on using a pink permanent felt marker with a diagonal point. Other cheeks have been embroidered by making a small line with two strands of yarn or thread at the bottom outside corner of each eye. The material necessary to draw or embroider the cheeks (felt marker or 10in [25cm] of pink thread) is not indicated at the start of each design. It is up to you whether or not to make these cheeks.

Head

Crochet in a spiral.
Rnd 1: 6 sc in a magic circle (6 st).
Rnd 2: 6 inc (12 st).
Rnd 3: (1 sc, 1 inc) x 6 (18 st).
Rnd 4: (1 sc, 1 inc, 1 sc) x 6 (24 st).
Rnd 5: (7 sc, 1 inc) x 3 (27 st).
Rnd 6: (3 sc, 1 inc, 5 sc) x 3 (30 st).
Rnds 7 to 10: 30 sc (30 st).
Rnd 11: (3 sc, 1 dec) x 6 (24 st).

For the **duck, cat, elephant, koala, rabbit, lion:** Insert the safety eyes between rnds 9 and 10, in st 12 and 19 of rnd 9.
For the **pig, dinosaur, unicorn:** Insert the safety eyes between rnds 8 and 9, in st 12 and 19 of rnd 8.
Sew the ears and/or other elements of the head as indicated for each animal.
Start to stuff the head.
Rnd 12: (1 sc, 1 dec, 1 sc) x 6 (18 st).
Rnd 13: (1 dec, 1 sc) x 5, 1 dec, 1 sc (12 st).
Cut the yarn to a length of 12in (30cm).
Finish stuffing the head. Sew the last elements and/or embroider the nose, the whiskers, or the eyebrows as indicated for each animal.

BODY

Front legs

To be done for the following animals: **cat, pig, dinosaur, squirrel, elephant, fawn, koala, unicorn, rabbit, lion, fox, tiger, cow.**
Cut a piece of yarn to a length of 8in (20cm). Fold this yarn in half and make an overhand knot so as to obtain a small loop in the middle of the yarn, about 1/5in (5mm) in length.

Back legs

Design A: For the **duck, cat, pig, dinosaur, squirrel, elephant, fawn, koala, unicorn, rabbit, lion, fox, tiger, cow:** Crochet 5 sc in a magic circle, keeping 4in (10cm) of yarn at the start and 6in (15cm) at the end.

Design B: For the **parakeet, penguin**: Make the two feet by following the instructions for the front legs.

Body

Crochet in the round, in closed rnds. The sl st that closes each rnd and the ch that starts each rnd are not indicated in the instructions, for better readability, but you must make them for each rnd. For more instructions, see the *Techniques* chapter, p. 22.

Rnd 1: 6 sc in a magic circle (6 st).
Rnd 2: 6 inc (12 st).
Rnd 3: (1 sc, 1 inc) x 6 (18 st).
Rnd 4: (1 sc, 1 inc, 1 sc) x 6 (24 st).
Rnd 5: 24 st in the BLO (24 st).
Rnds 6 to 9: 24 sc (24 st).

Design A: Attach the back legs to the body as follows: Using a needle, with the yarn left at the end, sew the 1st and last sc of the 1st leg in st 8 and 10 of rnd 5 (between rnds 4 and 5), and tie the starting and ending yarns of the leg in a knot several times on the inside of the body, tightening the knots well. Sew the second leg at the level of st 15 and 17 of rnd 5.

Design B: Attach the back legs to the body as follows: Using a needle, thread the 2 yarns of the 1st leg in st 9 and 10 of rnd 5 (between rnds 4 and 5) and knot them several times on the inside of the body, tightening the knots well. Thread the yarns of the 2nd leg through st 15 and 16 of rnd 5.

Rnd 10: (1 sc, 1 dec, 1 sc) x 6 (18 st).
Rnd 11: (1 sc, 1 dec) x 6 (12 st).
Cut the yarn to a length of 4in (10cm). Do not close it yet.
Continue by following the instructions for **Assembly**, below.

ASSEMBLY

For the **duck, cat, pig, dinosaur, squirrel, elephant, fawn, koala, unicorn, rabbit, lion, parakeet, cow:** Mark the 3rd st of rnd 11 of the body.
For the **penguin, fox, tiger:** Mark the 2nd st of rnd 11 of the body.
Attach the front legs to the body for the animals concerned. Using a needle, thread both yarns of the 1st leg through st 8 and 9 of rnd 9 (between rnds 9 and 10) and knot them several times on the inside of the body, tightening the knots well. Thread the yarns of the 2nd leg through st 17 and 18 of rnd 9.

Sew the other elements of the body (tail, wings, belly, etc.) according to the instructions given for each animal.
Close the body by stopping the yarn invisibly. Tie the yarn in a knot on the inside and cut it off.

Stuff the body using plastic pellets. The idea is to stuff sufficiently so that the body does not sag. However, you must not overstuff it; otherwise, the form of the body will be slightly stretched and the base will no longer be flat.

Sew the head to the body, using the yarn that you kept at the end of the head. Start by inserting the needle in the st marked on the last rnd of the body, from the inside to the outside. Next, insert the needle in the preceding st of the head (next-to-last stitch of rnd 13), from the outside to the inside. Sew all around, repeating these two steps.

Before making the last stitches, adjust some stuffing pellets, if necessary. Once the last stitch has been made, insert the needle in the neck and bring it out on the opposite side, also at the level of the neck. Then insert the needle just to one side and bring it out at the level of the neck again. Then insert the needle just to one side and bring it out at the level of the magic circle of the body. Insert the needle just beside the magic circle and bring it out at the level of the neck again. Take the time to give a good shape to the body and to adjust the tension of the yarn: this yarn must maintain the base of the body nice and flat and keep it from becoming rounded, but without pulling it toward the center so much that it creates a hollow space. To finish, make some more stitches in the head to secure the yarn and cut it off flush with the surface.

Lion

 2 hours 45 minutes

 pp. 6, 8

Dimensions
Approximate height: 2¾in (7cm)

Materials
- One 2.25mm crochet hook
- DMC Happy Cotton (¾oz–47yd [20g–43m]), shade 794, mustard, 4/10oz (11g); shade 777, brown, 1/7oz (4g)
- Two 6mm (¼in) safety eyes
- Chenille stem, 2in (5cm) (optional)

EARS X 2

In mustard. Crochet in a spiral.
Rnd 1: 5 sc in a magic circle (5 st).
Rnd 2: 5 inc (10 st).
Rnd 3: (2 sc, 1 dec, 1 sc) x 2 (8 st).
Rnd 4: 1 sc, do not crochet the other st of the rnd (8 st).
Cut the yarn to a length of 10in (25cm). Flatten each ear so as to have the yarn at one end and curve the ear slightly inward.

MANE

In brown.
Ch 46, keeping 4in (10cm) of starting yarn; 1 dc in the 4th st away from the crochet hook, 4 more dc in the same st, skip the next st of the ch; (5 dc in the next st, skip the following st of the ch) x 20; 5 dc in the next st, 3 ch, 1 sl st in the same st as the last 5 dc.
Cut the yarn to a length of 16in (40cm).

HEAD

In mustard, follow the instructions for the Head in *Basic Shapes*, p. 28.
After rnd 11, sew the ears straddling rnds 4 to 6, curving them slightly inward. The base of the right ear is sewn in the 4th and 5th st toward the outside from the right eye, 3 rnds above the line of the eyes. The base of the left ear is sewn in the 3rd and 4th st toward the outside from the left eye, on the same line as the other ear. Tie the yarns in a knot on the inside of the head and cut them off.
Sew the mane on with the yarn kept at the end. Insert the needle on the line of the eyes, under the right ear. Bring the needle out 1 rnd higher, run the yarn through the ch in which you made the 5 next-to-last dc and insert the needle in the same place in the head.
Bring the needle out 1 rnd higher, toward the back of the ear, skip 1 ch on the mane, and insert the needle in the following ch that contains 5 dc, insert the needle in the same place on the head. Continue like this 5 more times, passing behind the ear, until you come to rnds 2 and 3 of the head. Next, make stitches in each one of the st between rnds 2 and 3, until you are behind the top of the left ear (7 additional sewing stitches). The mane forms an arch at the top of the head. Come back down behind the left ear and then to the line of the eyes, making 7 more stitches. Tie the yarn in a knot on the inside of the head and cut it off. Using a needle, bring the starting yarn to the inside, tie it in a knot, and cut it off. Finish crocheting the head.
With 8in (20cm) of brown yarn, embroider the lion's nose as indicated below, making the top line at the same level as the eyes:

If you wish, embroider or draw cheeks according to the instructions given in *Basic Shapes*, p. 28.

TAIL

In mustard. Crochet in a spiral.
Rnd 1: 4 sc in a magic circle (4 st).
Rnd 2: 1 inc, 3 sc (5 st).

Rnd 3: 5 sc (5 st).
Cut 3 lengths of brown yarn 4in (10cm) long and tie them together at one end with an overhand knot. Using a needle, insert the long side of the 3 yarns in the magic circle of the tail, from the inside to the outside. The knot must be at the end of the tail, with the 3 yarns sticking out. Pull these yarns until the knot rests against the magic circle and continue crocheting.
Rnds 4 to 6: 5 sc (5 st).
Rnd 7: 4 sc, 1 sl st (5 st).
Cut the brown yarns to a length of about ½in (1cm), separate the strands of each yarn, to give a "feather duster" effect.

Optional: To stiffen the tail, take a pipe cleaner and fold one end in, approximately half an inch down, with your fingers or pliers. Insert the pipe cleaner into the tail all the way until the end, and trim the excess, leaving ½in (1cm) remaining. Pull the pipe cleaner out slightly so you can fold over the remaining end, and insert it back into the tail.

BODY

In mustard, follow the instructions for the Body in *Basic Shapes*, p. 28.
Sew the tail to the back side, straddling rnds 5 and 6 of the body. Tie the yarn in a knot on the inside and cut it off.

Koala

Dimensions

Approximate height: 1¾in (4.5cm)

Materials

- One 2.25mm crochet hook
- DMC Happy Cotton (¾oz–47yd [20g–43m]), shade 757, pearl gray, 4/10oz (11g); shade 762, white, 3¼yd (3m); shade 7754, black, 39in (1m)
- Two 6mm (¼in) safety eyes

EARS X 2

Inside part x 2
In white.
5 sc in a magic circle. Cut the yarn to a length of 4in (10cm). Using a needle, thread the yarn under both loops of the 1st st made in the magic circle, from the back to the front.
Then thread this yarn under the BL of the last st made in the circle, from the front to the back. Tie this yarn to the starting yarn and cut it off. You now have a closed circle with 6 st.
Outside part x 2
In gray. Crochet in a spiral.
Rnd 1: 6 sc in a magic circle (6 st).
Rnd 2: Crochet both parts simultaneously, positioning the white circle over the gray one. Insert the crochet hook in the BLO of the st of the white part, and in both loops of the gray part. Crochet the rnd as follows: 5 inc, 1 sc (11 st).
Rnd 3: (1 inc, 1 sc) x 4, 1 sc and 1 sl st in the same st. Do not crochet the last st. Mark the 2nd st of rnd 3 (16 st).
Cut the yarn to a length of 10in (25cm). If the starting yarn is still visible, bring the gray starting yarn to the inside of the ear and cut it off flush with the surface.

NOSE

In black.

In a magic circle, keeping 4in (10cm) of starting yarn, crochet: 1 sc, 1 hdc, 2 sc, 1 hdc. Cut the yarn to a length of 10in (25cm).

Using a needle, thread this yarn under both loops of the 1st st made in the magic circle, from back to front. Then thread this yarn under the BL of the last st made in the circle, from front to back. That forms 2 loops, replacing the 6th st. Keep the yarns to sew the nose.

HEAD

In gray, follow the instructions for the head in *Basic Shapes*, p. 28.

After rnd 11, sew on the ears as follows:

Count 4 st toward the outside of each eye and 1 row above to locate the position for the bottom of each ear. The upper end of each ear is placed 5 rnds higher on the head, directly above this point. The st previously marked on each ear is the last st sewn at the other extremity of the ear. Make sewing stitches every 2 st at the extremities of each ear and every 3 st between them.

To keep the ears from bending forward, make 1 or 2 stitches in a st at the back of each ear to keep them in place. Tie a knot in the yarn on the inside of the head and cut it off.

Finish crocheting the head.

Sew the nose between the two eyes, straddling rnds 9 and 10 of the head, positioning the oval vertically. If you wish, embroider or draw cheeks according to the instructions given in *Basic Shapes*, p. 28.

BELLY

In white. Crochet in a spiral.

Rnd 1: 6 sc in a magic circle (6 st).

Rnd 2: (1 inc, 1 hdc and 1 dc in 1 st, 1 dc and 1 hdc in 1 st) x 2 (12 st).

Rnd 3: 1 sl st, do not crochet the other st (12 st).

Cut the yarn to a length of 10in (25cm).

BODY

In gray, follow the instructions for the Body in *Basic Shapes*, p. 28.

Sew the belly over rnds 5 to 10 of the body. Tie the yarn in a knot on the inside and cut the yarn.

Elephant

2 hours 30 minutes

pp. 6, 7

Dimensions

Approximate height: 2⅓in (6cm)

Materials

- One 2.25 mm crochet hook
- DMC Happy Cotton (¾oz–47yd [20g–43m]), shade 759, pebble gray, 4/10 oz (11g); shade 764, chamallow pink, 2¼yd (2m)
- Two 6mm (¼in) safety eyes

EARS X 2

Inside part x 2

In pink. Crochet in a spiral.

Rnd 1: 6 sc in a magic circle (6 st).

Rnd 2: 6 inc (12 st).

Cut the yarn and stop it invisibly.

Exterior part x 2

In gray. Crochet in a spiral.

Rnd 1: 6 sc in a magic circle (6 st).
Rnd 2: 6 inc (12 st).
Rnd 3: Crochet the 2 parts simultaneously, positioning the pink part over the gray part: insert the crochet hook in 1 st of the pink part, then in the 1st st of rnd 2 of the gray part, and continue like that for the entire row: (1 inc, 1 sc) x 4, 1 sc and 1 sl st in the same st. Do not crochet the last st. Mark the 1st st of rnd 3 (17 st).
Cut the yarn to a length of 10in (25cm). If necessary, pull the starting yarn of the gray part to the inside of the ear and cut it off flush with the surface.

TRUNK

In gray. Crochet in a spiral.
Rnd 1: 6 sc in a magic circle (6 st).
Rnds 2 and 3: 6 sc (6 st).
Rnd 4: 2 sc, 1 dec, 1 sc, 1 inc (6 st).
Rnd 5: 1 sc, 1 dec, 1 sc, 2 inc (7 st).
Rnd 6: 1 sc, 1 sl st, do not crochet the last st (7 st).
Cut the yarn to a length of 8in (20cm). Do not stuff.

HEAD

In gray, follow the instructions for the Head in *Basic Shapes*, p. 28.
After rnd 11, sew the ears as follows: Count 4 st toward the outside of each eye to find the position for the lower end of each ear. The upper end of each ear is placed 5 rnds higher on the head, straight up from the lower end. The st marked previously on each ear is the last st sewn at the other end of the ear. Make sewing stitches every 2 st at the ends of each ear. To sew the 3 st between the two ends, insert the needle in both the pink part and the gray part of each ear. To keep the ears from folding toward the front, make 1 or 2 stitches in a st at the back of each ear to keep them in place. Tie the yarn in a knot on the inside of the head and cut it off.
Finish crocheting the head.
Sew the trunk between the 2 eyes, straddling rnds 10 and 11 of the head, making sure that it is curved in the right direction. If you wish, embroider or draw cheeks according to the instructions given in *Basic Shapes*, p. 28.

TAIL

In gray.
Ch 3, keeping ¾in (1.5cm) of starting yarn. Tighten the starting knot well.
Cut the yarn to a length of 6in (15cm). Separate the strands of the starting yarn to give a "feather duster" effect.

BODY

In gray, follow the instructions for the Body in *Basic Shapes*, p. 28.
Once the body is finished, sew the tail to the back side, between rnds 4 and 5: insert the needle in the 1st st of rnd 5, from the outside to the inside of the body, and bring the needle out beside it, in the last st of rnd 5. Insert the needle in the 3rd ch of the tail, from the front to the back, and insert the needle in the body again, between the 2 sewing stitches. Knot the yarn on the inside and cut it off.

Parakeet

 2 hours 15 minutes

 pp. 6, 9

Dimensions
Approximate height: 2⅓in (6cm)

Materials
- One 2.25 mm crochet hook
- DMC Happy Cotton (¾oz–47yd [20g–43m]), **for the red design:** shade 789, red, ⅓oz (9g); shade 788, lemon yellow, 2¼yd (2m); shade 786, cyan blue, 60in (1.5m); shade 781, malachite green, 2¾yd (2.5m); shade 762, white, 10in (25cm); **for the blue design:** shade 786, cyan blue, ⅓oz (9g); shade 788, lemon yellow, 5½yd (5m); shade 781, malachite green, 60in (1.5m); shade 762, white, 10in (25cm)
- Two 6mm (¼in) safety eyes

BEAK

In yellow. Crochet in a spiral.
Rnd 1: 6 sc in a magic circle (6 st).
Rnd 2: 3 sc, 2 inc, 1 sc (8 st).
Rnd 3: 8 sc (8 st).
Rnd 4: 1 sl st, do not crochet the other st (8 st).
Cut the yarn to a length of 10in (25cm). Stuff.

FEATHERS

In red (or in blue).
Ch 2, keeping 4in (10cm) of starting yarn; 1 sl st in the 2nd st away from the crochet hook. Continue by making a new ch of ch 4; 1 inc (2 sc) in the 2nd st away from the crochet hook, 2 sl st continuing along the ch.
Cut the yarn to a length of 6in (15cm).
This forms 2 feathers (1 small and 1 a little longer) that will be sewn to the top of the head.

HEAD

In red (or in blue). Crochet in a spiral.
Rnd 1: 6 sc in a magic circle (6 st).
Rnd 2: 6 inc (12 st).
Rnd 3: (1 sc, 1 inc) x 6 (18 st).
Rnd 4: (4 sc, 1 inc, 1 sc) x 3 (21 st).
Rnd 5: (1 sc, 1 inc, 5 sc) x 3 (24 st).
Rnd 6: (7 sc, 1 inc) x 3 (27 st).
Rnd 7: (3 sc, 1 inc, 5 sc) x 3 (30 st).
Rnds 8 to 10: 30 sc (30 st).
Rnd 11: (3 sc, 1 dec) x 6 (24 st).
Insert the safety eyes between rnds 9 and 10, in st 12 and 19 of rnd 9.
Use the yarn from the end of the feathers to sew the feathers to the top of the head, straddling the 1st rnd, placing the small feather in front of the larger one.
Bring the starting yarn to the inside, tie both yarns on the inside of the head, and cut them off.
Start stuffing the head.
Rnd 12: (1 sc, 1 dec, 1 sc) x 6 (18 st).
Rnd 13: (1 dec, 1 sc) x 5, 1 dec, 1 sl st (12 st).
Cut the yarn to a length of 12in (30cm).
Finish stuffing the head.
Sew the beak between the two eyes, straddling rnds 10 to 12 of the head. So that it sits in the right place, the ending yarn must be on the side of the parakeet's left eye. If necessary, adjust the stuffing in the beak before making the last stitches.
With the white yarn, embroider the eyebrows (see the photo). If you wish, embroider or draw the cheeks according to the instructions given in *Basic Shapes*, p. 28.

WINGS X 2

In green (or in yellow). Crochet in a spiral.
Rnd 1: 6 sc in a magic circle (6 st).
Rnd 2: (1 sc, 1 hdc, 1 dc) in 1 st, mark the hdc, (1 dc, 1 hdc, 1 sc) in the next st. Do not crochet the other st (10 st).

Cut the yarn to a length of 10in (25cm). Stop it invisibly and keep the remaining yarn to sew the wing to the body.
In blue (or in green).
Pull a yarn through the st marked in rnd 2, keeping 4in (10cm) of starting length, and crochet as follows: Ch 1; (1 sc, 1 hdc, 1 dc) in the following st; ch 2, 1 sl st in the 2nd st away from the crochet hook; (1 dc, 1 hdc, 1 sc) in the next green (or yellow) st; 1 sl st in the following st.
Cut the yarn to a length of 4in (10cm). Stop this yarn and the starting yarn by making an invisible knot and pulling the ends under a few st before cutting the yarn off flush with the surface.

BODY

Make the body in red (or in blue) and the back legs in lemon yellow, following the instructions for the Body in *Basic Shapes*, p. 28.
Sew the wings on each side of the body. They must be positioned just outside each rear leg, with the green (or yellow) magic circle straddling rnds 8 to 10 of the body, and slanted so that the blue (or green) point is toward the bottom and back of the body. With the green (or yellow) ending yarn, sew all around the green (or yellow) part. The blue (or green) part of the wings remains free. Knot the yarn on the inside of the body and cut it off.

Tiger

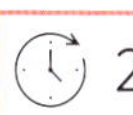 2 hours 45 minutes

 pp. 6, 7

Dimensions
Approximate height:
2⅓in (6cm)

Preliminary information
The head and the body are crocheted in the round, in closed rounds. The sl st that closes each rnd and the ch that starts each rnd are not indicated in the instructions, for better readability, **but you must make them for each rnd.** For more instructions, see the *Techniques* chapter, p. 22.
The color changes indicated at the end of a rnd for the head and the body should be made when making the **last sc** of the rnd, which means that the sl st that ends the rnd and the ch that start the next rnd will be made in the new color. This makes it possible to have invisible color changes.

Materials
- One 2.25mm crochet hook
- DMC Happy Cotton (¾oz–47yd [20g–43m]), shade 792, orange, $^{4}/_{10}$oz (11g); shade 775, black, $^{7}/_{100}$oz (2g); shade 762, white, 2¼yd (2m)
- Two 6mm (¼in) safety eyes
- Chenille stem, 2in (5cm) (optional)

EARS X 2

In orange, make 6 sc in a magic circle, keeping 4in (10cm) of starting and ending yarn.
In black, pull a yarn through the 1st st made in orange, keeping 4in (10cm) of starting yarn. Make ch 1 to start, then 1 sc in each of the 6 orange st.
Cut the yarn to a length of 6in (15cm).

MUZZLE

In white. Crochet in a spiral.
Rnd 1: 6 sc in a magic circle (6 st).
Rnd 2: 1 inc, 2 sc, 1 sc, and 1 sl st in the same st.
Do not crochet the last st (8 st).
Cut the yarn to a length of 10in (25cm).

HEAD

In orange. Crochet in the round, in closed rnds.
Rnd 1: 6 sc in a magic circle (6 st).
Rnd 2: 6 inc (12 st).
Rnd 3: (1 sc, 1 inc) x 2, 2 sc; in black: 1 sc in the same st as the preceding one, 1 sc;
in orange: (1 inc, 1 sc) x 2, 1 inc (18 st).
Rnd 4: (1 sc, 1 inc, 1 sc) x 6. Change color to black (24 st).
Rnd 5: 5 sc; in orange: 2 sc, 1 inc, 2 sc;
in black: 4 sc; in orange: 1 sc, 1 inc, 3 sc;
in black: 4 sc, 1 inc. Change color to orange (27 st).
Rnd 6: (3 sc, 1 inc, 5 sc) x 3. Change color to black (30 st).
Rnd 7: 8 sc; in orange: 14 sc; in black: 8 sc. Change color to orange (30 sc).
Rnd 8: 30 sc. Change color to black (30 st).
Rnds 9 and 10: Repeat rnds 7 and 8 (30 st).
Rnd 11: 3 sc, 1 dec; in orange: (3 sc, 1 dec) x 4; in black: 3 sc, 1 dec. Change color to orange (24 st).
Insert the safety eyes between rnds 9 and 10, in st 12 and 19 of rnd 9.
Sew the ears on each side of the head, straddling rnds 4 and 5. First sew the orange part, tie the yarns on the inside of the head, and cut off. Then pull the black yarns at the end of each ear to the inside, tie them in a knot and cut them off.
Start to stuff the head.
Rnd 12: (1 sc, 1 dec, 1 sc) x 6 (18 st).
Rnd 13: (1 dec, 1 sc) x 5, 1 dec, 1 sl st (12 st).
Cut the yarn to a length of 12in (30cm).
Finish stuffing the head. Sew the muzzle between the two eyes, straddling rnds 10 and 11 of the head. The 2 st of the magic circle that were not crocheted in rnd 2 of the muzzle must be positioned toward the top.
With the black yarn, embroider a small horizontal line just above the magic circle of the muzzle.
If you wish, embroider or draw the cheeks according to the instructions given in *Basic Shapes*, p. 28.

TAIL

In black. Crochet in a spiral.
Rnd 1: 4 sc in a magic circle (4 st).
Rnd 2: 1 inc, 3 sc (5 st).
Rnd 3: 5 sc (5 st)
Rnd 4: In orange. 5 sc (5 st).
Rnd 5: In black. 5 sc (5 st).
Rnds 6 and 7: Repeat rnds 4 and 5 (5 st).
Rnd 8: In orange. 4 sc, 1 sl st (5 st).
Stop the black yarn and cut the orange yarn to a length of 8in (20cm).
Optional: To stiffen the tail, take a pipe cleaner and fold one end in, approximately half an inch down, with your fingers or pliers. Insert the pipe cleaner into the tail all the way until the end, and trim the excess, leaving ½in (1cm) remaining. Pull the pipe cleaner out slightly so you can fold over the remaining end, and insert it back into the tail.

BELLY

In white. Crochet in a spiral.
Rnd 1: 6 sc in a magic circle (6 st).
Rnd 2: 6 inc (12 st).
Rnd 3: 1 sl st, do not crochet the other st (12 st).
Cut the yarn to a length of 10in (25cm).

BODY

In orange. Crochet in the round, in closed rnds.
Rnd 1: 6 sc in a magic circle (6 st).
Rnd 2: 6 inc (12 st).

Rnd 3: (1 sc, 1 inc) x 6 (18 st).
Rnd 4: (1 sc, 1 inc, 1 sc) x 6 (24 st).
Rnd 5: 24 sc in the BLO. Change color to black (24 st).
Rnd 6: 8 sc; in orange: 8 sc; in black: 8 sc. Change color to orange (24 sc).
Rnd 7: 24 sc. Change color to black (24 sc).
Rnd 8: 6 sc; in orange: 12 sc; in black: 6 sc. Change color to orange (24 st).
Rnd 9: 24 sc. Change color to black (24 st).
In orange, make the back legs an attach them to the body as explained in the Body instructions in *Basic Shapes*, p. 28.
Rnd 10: 1 sc, 1 dec, 1 sc; in orange: (1 sc, 1 dec, 1 sc) x 4; in black: 1 sc, 1 dec, 1 sc. Change color to orange (18 st).
Rnd 11: (1 sc, 1 dec) x 6 (12 st).
Cut the yarn, keeping a length of 4in (10cm). Do not close for the time being.
Sew the tail to the back side, straddling rnds 5 and 6. Tie the yarn in a knot on the inside and cut it off.
Sew the belly over rnds 6 to 9 of the body. Tie a knot in the yarn on the inside and cut it off.
In orange, make the front legs and attach them to the body as explained in the Assembly section of *Basic Shapes*, p. 29. Then follow the rest of the instructions in that part to finish the tiger.

Alpaca

2 hours 45 minutes

pp. 6, 8

Dimensions
Approximate height: 3¾in (9.5cm)

Materials
- One 2.25mm crochet hook
- DMC Happy Cotton (¾oz–47yd [20g–43m]), shade 773, beige ⅓oz (9g); shade 761, ecru, 1/7oz (4g)
- DMC Lumina (¾oz–164yd [20g–150m]), shade L677, pink gold, 22yd (20m). Divide this length into three equal parts. Crochet the parts in pink gold by using these three yarns simultaneously, to have a thickness similar to that of Happy Cotton.
- DMC Pearl Cotton Size 5, shade 310, black, 8in (20cm)
- Two 4.5mm (1/5in) safety eyes

EARS X 2

In pink gold. Crochet in a spiral.
Rnd 1: 4 sc in a magic circle (4 st).
In beige.
Rnd 2: (1 inc, 1 sc) x 2 (6 st).
Rnds 3 and 4: 6 sc (6 st).
Rnd 5: 1 sl st. Do not crochet the other st (6 st).
Cut the yarn to a length of 8in (20cm). Flatten the ear so as to have this yarn at one end.

MUZZLE

In ecru. Crochet in a spiral.
Rnd 1: 5 sc in a magic circle (5 st).
Rnd 2: 5 inc (10 st).
Rnd 3: 10 sc (10 st).
Rnd 4: 4 sc, 1 sl st. Do not crochet the other st (10 st).
Cut the yarn to a length of 10in (25cm).

HEAD AND BODY

Head

In beige. Crochet in a spiral.

Rnd 1: 6 sc in a magic circle (6 st).

Rnd 2: 6 inc (12 st).

Rnd 3: (1 sc, 1 inc) x 6 (18 st).

Rnd 4: (4 sc, 1 inc, 1 sc) x 3 (21 st).

Rnd 5: (1 sc, 1 inc, 5 sc) x 3 (24 st).

Rnds 6 to 8: 24 sc (24 st).

Insert the safety eyes between rnds 6 and 7, in st 9 and 16 of rnd 6.

Sew the ears on each side of the head, straddling rnds 2 and 3. Tie the yarns in knots on the inside and cut them off.

Rnd 9: (1 sc, 1 dec, 1 sc) x 6 (18 st).

Start to stuff the head.

Rnd 10: 9 dec (9 st).

Finish stuffing the head.

Neck

Rnds 11 to 16: 9 sc (9 st).

Stuff the neck as you go along.

Rnd 17: 8 sc; in the FLO: 1 inc (10 st).

Body

Rnd 18: FLO: 3 inc; in both loops: 2 sc, 1 inc, 2 sc, 2 inc (16 st).

Verify that the head and the start of the body are well aligned. Depending on an individual's way of crocheting, a slight offset can be created. The 4 inc in rnds 17 and 18 done in the FL should be done at the back of the body, well centered with respect to the position of the eyes. If that is not the case, adjust or take out 1 sc in rnd 17 before making the inc. To avoid losing your place in the instructions, mark the 3rd st of the inc made in the FL as the 1st st of rnd 18.

Rnd 19: 6 inc, 10 sc (22 st).

Rnd 20: 14 sc, 2 dec, 4 sc (20 st).

Rnd 21: 1 sc, 7 inc, 12 sc (27 st).

Rnds 22 and 23: 27 sc (27 st).

Rnd 24: 19 sc, 3 dec, 2 sc (24 st).

Rnd 25: (1 dec, 6 sc) x 3 (21 st).

Rnd 26: 1 sc, 7 dec, 6 sc (14 st).

Start to stuff the body.

Rnd 27: 7 dec (7 st).

Finish stuffing and close.

LEGS X 4

In pink gold. Crochet in a spiral.

Rnd 1: 4 sc in a magic circle (4 st).

Rnd 2: 1 inc, 3 sc (5 st).

Rnd 3: 1 inc, 4 sc (6 st).

Rnd 4: 1 sl st. Do not crochet the other st (6 st).

Cut the yarn, keeping a length of 10in (25cm).

TAIL

In beige.

Ch 3, keeping 6in (15cm) of starting yarn; 1 sl st in the 2nd st away from the crochet hook, 1 sc in the next st.

Cut the yarn to a length of 6in (15cm).

ASSEMBLY

Position the four legs using pins before sewing them, to make sure that the alpaca is not wobbly. I place the front legs on each side of the neck (leaving a gap of 2 to 3 st between them), straddling rnds 23 and 24 of the body. The hind legs are placed straddling rnds 25 and 26, about 3 st behind the front legs.

Sew each leg, adding a little stuffing before making the last stitch.

Sew the tail between the two hind legs, between rnds 22 and 23 of the body.

Sew the muzzle between the two eyes, across rnds 6 to 9. Stuff lightly before making the last stitches. With 8in (20cm) of black Pearl Cotton, embroider a Y on the muzzle of the alpaca, with the intersection of the 3 branches at the magic circle of the muzzle. If you wish, embroider or draw cheeks according to the instructions given in *Basic Shapes*, p. 28.

Unicorn

 3 hours 15 minutes

 p. 10

Dimensions

Approximate height: 3⅛in (8cm)

Materials

- One 2.25mm crochet hook
- DMC Happy Cotton (¾oz–47yd [20g–43m]), shade 762, white, 4/10oz (11g); shade 783, water green, 1/10oz (3g); shade 764, chamallow pink, 24in (60cm); shade 763, layette pink, 3¼yd (3m)
- DMC Lumina (¾oz–164yd [20g–150m]), shade L3821, golden, 4¾yd (4.2m)
- DMCPearl Cotton Size 5, shade 310, black, 16in (40cm)
- Two 6mm (¼in) safety eyes

EARS X 2

In white. Crochet in a spiral.

Rnd 1: 4 sc in a magic circle (4 st).

Rnd 2: (1 inc, 1 sc) x 2 (6 st).

Rnd 3: (1 inc, 1 sc) x 3 (9 st).

Rnd 4: 9 sc (9 st).

Rnd 5: 4 dec, 1 sl st (5 st).

Cut the yarn to a length of 8in (20cm). Flatten the ear so as to have the yarn at one end.

With the chamallow pink yarn, embroider 2 small vertical lines, 2 rnds high, in the middle of each ear. I prefer to embroider them on the side of the 2nd and 3rd st of rnd 5 so that the ear is sewn in the right direction. Tie the yarns in a knot, cut them off, and pull them back into the ear.

HORN

In white. Crochet in a spiral. Stuff as you go along.

Rnd 1: 4 sc in a magic circle (4 st).

Crochet all the following rnds in the BLO.

Rnd 2: 1 inc, 3 sc (5 st).

Rnd 3: 2 sc, 1 inc, 2 sc (6 st).

Rnd 4: 6 sc (6 st).

Rnd 5: 2 sc, 1 sl st in both loops of the st.

Do not crochet the last st (6 st).

Cut the yarn to a length of 8in (20cm).

With a gold yarn, make a gold edging all around the horn, in the FL, working upward in a spiral: insert the needle, from the bottom of the horn toward the top, in each FL, starting with the last one. Bring both ends of the yarn to the inside, make a knot, and hide the yarns in the stuffing.

MUZZLE

In layette pink. Crochet in a spiral.

Rnd 1: 6 sc in a magic circle (6 st).

Rnd 2: (1 inc, 1 sc) x 3 (9 st).

Rnd 3: (1 sc, 1 inc, 1 sc) x 3 (12 st).

Rnd 4: 12 sc (12 st).

Rnd 5: 6 sc, 1 sl st. Do not crochet the other st (12 st).

Cut the yarn to a length of 12in (30cm).

MANE

In green. Crochet in a spiral. Do not stuff.

Rnd 1: 6 sc in a magic circle (6 st).

Rnds 2 to 15: 6 sc (6 st).

Cut the yarn to a length of 16in (40cm). Close and keep the yarn for sewing.

HEAD

In white, follow the instructions for the Head in *Basic Shapes*, p. 28.

After rnd 11, before attaching the washers to the backs of the safety eyes, embroider 2 small lines in black Pearl Cotton, toward the outside of each eye. Each black eyelash starts from the st in which the safety eye is inserted and goes diagonally, 1 st toward the outside and 1 st upward. Then attach

the washers to the backs of the safety eyes.
Sew the ears on each side of the head, over rnd 4. Tie the yarns in a knot on the inside and cut them off.
Sew the horn between the eyes, over rnd 4 of the head, extending a little over rnds 3 and 5. Tie the yarn in a knot and cut it off.
Finish crocheting the head.
Sew the muzzle between the 2 eyes, straddling rnds 9 to 12 of the head. Stuff before making the last sewing stitches.
Sew the mane on with the yarn kept at the end. The bottom of the mane should end between rnds 12 and 13, at the back of the head, and the top should start between rnds 2 and 3 in the front of the head, just behind the horn. Make several sewing stitches along the center of the mane, without tightening too much, so as not to crush it.
If you wish, embroider or draw cheeks according to the instructions given in the *Basic Shapes* section, p. 28.

TAIL

In green. Crochet in a spiral.
Rnd 1: 4 sc in a magic circle (4 st).
Rnd 2: 4 sc (4 st).
Rnd 3: 2 inc, 2 sc (6 st).
Rnd 4: 3 inc, 2 sc, 1 inc (10 st).
Rnd 5: 10 sc (10 st).
Start stuffing.
Rnd 6: 5 dec (5 st).
Rnd 7: 1 sl st. Do not crochet the other st (5 st).
Cut the yarn to a length of 8in (20cm). Finish stuffing.

BODY

Make the body in white and the front legs with 3 gold yarns tied together, following the instructions given in the *Basic Shapes* section, p. 28.
Make each hind leg using 3 lengths of gold yarn simultaneously, each one 24in (60cm) long, to have a thickness similar to that of Happy Cotton.
Sew the tail at the back, straddling rnds 5 and 6 of the body. Tie the yarn in a knot on the inside and cut it.
With chamallow pink yarn, embroider a small cross in the middle of the belly over rnd 7, to suggest a navel.

Dinosaur

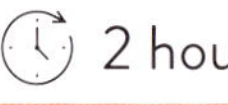
2 hours

p. 11

Dimensions
Approximate height: 2¾in (7cm)

Materials
- One 2.25mm crochet hook
- DMC Happy Cotton (¾oz–47yd [20g–43m]), shade 782, almond green, 4/10oz (11g); shade 788, lemon yellow, 2¾yd (2.5m)
- Two 6mm (¼in) safety eyes

CREST

In yellow.
Ch 15, keeping 6in (15cm) of starting yarn. The 1st sc of the following instructions must be made in the 2nd st away from the crochet hook: *2 sc, turn the work; ch 1, 2 sc in the 2 sc that you just crocheted, turn; 1 ch, skip the 1st st and make 1 sc in the following st; make 2 sl st to go back down the peak you just made*; 2 sl st on the starting ch. Repeat the instructions from * to * 3 times more, to make 4 peaks in all, inserting 2 sl st on the starting ch between each peak. The 4th peak must

end on the last st remaining of the starting ch. Finish by making 1 sl st.
Cut the yarn to a length of 16in (40cm).

MUZZLE

In green. Crochet in a spiral.
Rnd 1: 6 sc in a magic circle (6 st).
Rnd 2: 6 inc (12 st).
Rnd 3: (1 sc, 1 dec, 1 sc) x 3 (9 st).
Rnd 4: 1 sl st. Do not crochet the other st (9 st).
Cut the yarn to a length of 10in (25cm).

HEAD

In green, follow the instructions for the Head in *Basic Shapes*, p. 28.
Sew the muzzle between the 2 eyes, straddling rnds 9 to 11 of the head. Stuff it before making the last sewing stitches.
Use the ending yarn from the crest to sew the crest on the head.
Insert the needle in the front of the head, between the eyes, between rnds 2 and 3. Bring the needle out at the back of the head, in the middle, 3 rnds under the line of the eyes. Make 1 sewing stitch at the back end of the crest. Once the crest is positioned, sew the entire starting ch to the head, then bring the yarn out again under the head, through the stuffing.
Pull the starting yarn of the crest to the inside as well, tie the 2 yarns together, and cut them off.
If you wish, embroider or draw the cheeks according to the instructions given in the *Basic Shapes* section, p. 28.

TAIL

In green. Crochet in a spiral.
Rnd 1: 4 sc in a magic circle (4 st).
Rnd 2: (1 inc, 1 sc) x 2 (6 st).
Rnd 3: (1 sc, 1 inc, 1 sc) x 2 (8 st).
Rnd 4: (3 sc, 1 inc) x 2 (10 st).
Rnd 5: 1 inc, 6 sc, 1 inc, 2 sc (12 st).
Rnd 6: 12 sc (12 st).
Rnd 7: 1 sc, 1 inc, 6 sc, 1 inc, 3 sc (14 st).
Rnd 8: 4 sc, 1 sl st. Do not crochet the other st (14 st).
Cut the yarn to a length of 12in (30cm). Stuff.

BODY

In green, follow the instructions in the *Basic Shapes* section, p. 28.
Sew the tail to the back, over rnds 5 to 9 of the body. If necessary, add a bit of stuffing before making the last stitches. Tie the yarn in a knot on the inside and cut it off.
With 20in (50cm) of yellow yarn and a needle, embroider 4 horizontal lines on the back of the tail. The 1st line is placed between rnds 10 and 11 of the body and extends across the width of the tail. The 2nd one is placed on top of the tail, centered, between rnds 6 and 7, and is 4 st wide. The 3rd line is placed between rnds 4 and 5 of the tail and extends over 3 st of width. The last one is placed between rnds 2 and 3 of the tail and extends over 2 st of width. Tie the starting and ending yarns in a knot on the inside and cut them off.

Duck

1 hour 45 minutes

pp. 12, 13

Dimensions

Approximate height: 2⅓in (6cm)

Materials

› One 2.25mm crochet hook
› DMC Happy Cotton (¾oz–47yd [20g–43m]), shade 781, malachite green, ¼oz (6g); shade 777, brown, ⅐oz (4g); shade 773, beige, 4½yd (4m); shade 761, ecru, 2¼yd (2m); shade 788, lemon yellow, 2¾yd (2.5m); shade 753, tangerine orange, 39in (1m)
› Two 6mm (¼in) safety eyes

BEAK

In yellow. Crochet in a spiral.
Rnd 1: 8 sc in a magic circle (8 st).
Rnd 2: 8 sc (8 st).
Rnd 3: 1 sl st. Do not crochet the other st (8 st).
Cut the yarn to a length of 8in (20cm). Flatten the beak so that the yarn is at one end.

HEAD

In green, follow the instructions for the Head in *Basic Shapes*, p. 28.
Sew the beak by placing it between the eyes, over rnd 10 of the head. Sew the two thicknesses of the beak simultaneously to the head, using 4 sewing stitches.
If you wish, embroider or draw cheeks according to the instructions given in *Basic Shapes*, p. 28.

WINGS X 2

In beige.
In a magic circle, keeping 4in (10cm) of starting yarn, make: ch 1, 1 hdc, 3 dc, 1 hdc, 1 sl st.
Cut the yarn to a length of 6in (15cm).

TAIL

In beige. Crochet in a spiral.
Rnd 1: 7 sc in a magic circle (7 st).
Rnd 2: 2 sc, 1 dec, 3 sc (6 st).
Rnd 3: 1 sl st. Do not crochet the other st (6 st).
Cut the yarn to a length of 8in (20cm). Flatten the tail so that the yarn is at one end.

BODY

Using the instructions for the Body in *Basic Shapes*, p. 28, make the body in brown, except for the last rnd (rnd 11), which must be made in ecru (the color change is done when making the last sc of rnd 10), and the feet, which are made in orange.
Sew the wings on each side of the body, over rnd 10. Make a sewing stitch in the 1st st and in the last st of each wing. Bring the starting yarn to the inside. Tie the starting yarn and the ending yarn together on the inside and cut them off.
Sew the tail to the back side, between rnds 4 and 5. Sew the two thicknesses of the tail simultaneously, making 3 sewing stitches. Tie the yarn in a knot on the inside and cut it off.

Duckling

 1 hour

 pp. 12, 13

Dimensions
Approximate height: 1¾in (4.5cm)

Materials
› One 2.25mm crochet hook
› DMC Happy Cotton (¾oz–47yd [20g–43m]), shade 788, lemon yellow, ¼oz (6g); shade 793, coral, 39in (1m)
› Two 4.5mm (1/5in) safety eyes

BEAK

In coral.
Rnd 1: 6 sc in a magic circle (6 st).
Rnd 2: 1 sl st. Do not crochet the other st (6 st).
Cut the yarn to a length of 6in (15cm). Fold the magic circle in half to form the beak.

HEAD

In yellow. Crochet in a spiral.
Rnd 1: 6 sc in a magic circle (6 st).
Rnd 2: 6 inc (12 st).
Rnd 3: (1 sc, 1 inc) x 6 (18 st).
Rnd 4: (4 sc, 1 inc, 1 sc) x 3 (21 st).
Rnd 5: (1 sc, 1 inc, 5 sc) x 3 (24 st).
Rnds 6 to 8: 24 sc (24 st).
Rnd 9: (1 sc, 1 dec, 1 sc) x 6 (18 st).
Insert the safety eyes between rnds 7 and 8, in st 10 and 15 of rnd 7.
Start to stuff the head.
Rnd 10: 9 dec (9 st).
Rnd 11: 1 sc. Do not crochet the other st (9 st).
Cut the yarn to a length of 12in (30cm).
Finish stuffing the head.
Sew the beak by placing it between the eyes, on rnd 8 of the head. Sew both thicknesses of the beak simultaneously to the head, making 3 sewing stitches.
If you wish, embroider or draw the cheeks according to the instructions given in the *Basic Shapes* section, p. 28.

WINGS X 2

In yellow.
In a magic circle, keeping 4in (10cm) of starting yarn, make: 1 sc, 3 hdc, 1 sl st.
Cut the yarn to a length of 6in (15cm).

FEET X 2

In coral.
Make a slip knot, keeping 4in (10cm) of starting yarn, 1 ch.
Cut the yarn to a length of 4in (10cm).

BODY

In yellow. Crochet in the round, in closed rounds. The sl st that closes each rnd and the ch that starts each rnd are not indicated in the instructions, for better readability, but you must make them for each rnd. For more instructions, see the *Techniques* chapter, p. 22.
Rnd 1: 7 sc in a magic circle (7 st).
Rnd 2: 7 inc (14 st).
Rnd 3: 14 sc in the BLO (14 st).
Rnds 4 and 5: 14 sc (14 st).
Attach the back legs to the body: using a needle, thread both yarns of the 1st leg through st 6 and 7 of rnd 4 (between rnds 3 and 4), and tie them together several times on the inside of the body, tightening the knots well. Thread the yarns of the 2nd leg through st 9 and 10 of rnd 5.
Rnd 6: (1 dec, 1 sc) x 4, 1 dec (9 st).
Cut the yarn, keeping 4in (10cm) of length. Do not

close the body yet. Mark the 2nd st of rnd 6. Sew the wings on each side of the body, over rnd 5. Make a sewing st in the 1st st and the last st of each wing. Bring the starting yarn to the inside. Tie the starting and ending yarns together on the inside and cut them off.

Continue by following the instructions for Assembly in *Basic Shapes*, p. 29.

Cow

 2 hours 15 minutes

 p. 12

Dimensions

Approximate height: 2⅝in (6.5cm)

Materials

› One 2.25mm crochet hook
› DMC Happy Cotton (¾oz–47yd [20g–43m]), shade 761, ecru ⅓oz (9g); shade 777, brown, 1/10oz (3g); shade 764, chamallow pink, 2¼yd (2m)
› Lumina (¾oz–164yd [20g–150m]), shade L677, pink gold, 5½yd (5m) Divide this length into three equal parts. Crochet the parts in pink gold by using these three yarns simultaneously, to have a thickness similar to that of Happy Cotton.
› Two 6mm (¼in) safety eyes

EARS X 2

One ear in ecru and one ear in brown.
Crochet in a spiral.
Rnd 1: 4 sc in a magic circle (4 st).
Rnd 2: (1 inc, 1 sc) x 2 (6 st).
Rnd 3: (1 inc, 1 sc) x 3 (9 st).
Rnd 4: 9 sc (9 st).
Rnd 5: 4 dec, 1 sl st (5 st).
Cut the yarn to a length of 8in (20cm). Flatten the ear so that the yarn is at one end.
With the pink gold yarn and a needle, embroider two small vertical lines, 2 rnds high, in the middle of each ear. I prefer to embroider them on the side of the 2nd and 3rd st of rnd 5 so that the ear will be sewn in the right direction. Tie the yarns in a knot, cut them off, and pull them inside the ear.

HORNS X 2

In pink gold. Crochet in a spiral.
Rnd 1: 4 sc in a magic circle (4 st).
Rnd 2: 1 inc, 3 sc (5 st).
Rnd 3: 1 sl st. Do not crochet the other st (5 st).
Cut the yarn to a length of 10in (25cm). Add a little stuffing to each horn.

MUZZLE

In pink. Crochet in a spiral.
Rnd 1: Ch 4, 1 sc in the 2nd st away from the crochet hook; continuing along the ch: 1 sc; in the last st of the ch: 3 sc; going back up the other side of the ch: 1 sc, 1 inc (8 st).
Rnd 2: 8 sc (8 st).
Rnd 3: 1 sl st. Do not crochet the other st (8 st).
Cut the yarn to a length of 10in (25cm).

HEAD

In ecru. Crochet in a spiral.
Rnd 1: 6 sc in a magic circle (6 st).
Rnd 2: 6 inc (12 st).
Rnd 3: (1 sc, 1 inc) x 6 (18 st).
Rnd 4: (1 sc, 1 inc, 1 sc) x 5; in brown: 2 sc; in ecru: 1 sc in the same st as the previous one, 1 sc (24 st).

Rnd 5: 6 sc; in brown: 2 sc; in ecru: 1 sc in the same st as the previous one, 7 sc, 1 inc, 4 sc; in brown: 3 sc; in ecru: 1 inc (27 st).
Rnd 6: 3 sc, 1 inc, 2 sc; in brown: 3 sc; in ecru: 3 sc, 1 inc, 8 sc, 1 inc, 1 sc; in brown: 3 sc; in ecru: 1 sc (30 st).
Rnd 7: 7 sc; in brown: 4 sc; in ecru: 19 sc (30 st).
Rnd 8: 8 sc; in brown: 2 sc; in ecru: 20 sc (30 st).
Rnd 9: 2 sc; in brown: 3 sc; in ecru: 25 sc (30 st).
Rnd 10: 3 sc; in brown: 3 sc; in ecru: 24 sc (30 st).
Rnd 11: 3 sc; in brown: 1 dec, 1 sc; in ecru: 2 sc, 1 dec, (3 sc, 1 dec) x 4 (24 st).
Insert the safety eyes between rnds 9 and 10, in st 12 and 19 of rnd 9.
Sew the ears on each side of the head, straddling rnds 5 and 6. Tie the yarns in a knot on the inside and cut them off.
Sew the horns over rnd 3 of the head, between the ears. Tie the yarns in a knot and cut them off.
Rnd 12: (1 sc, 1 dec, 1 sc) x 6 (18 st).
Start stuffing the head.
Rnd 13: (1 dec, 1 sc) x 5, 1 dec, 1 sl st (12 st).
Cut the yarn, keeping a length of 12in (30cm) for sewing.
Finish stuffing the head. Sew the muzzle by placing it between the eyes, straddling rnds 10 and 11 of the head. Stuff before making the last sewing stitches.
If you wish, embroider or draw the cheeks according to the instructions given in the *Basic Shapes* section, p. 28.

TAIL

In ecru.
Ch 6, keeping 4in (10cm) of starting yarn, 1 sl st in the 2nd st away from the crochet hook, 4 sc along the ch.
Cut the yarn to a length of 4in (10cm).
Cut an 8in (20cm) length of brown yarn. Thread it through the st at the end of the ch (on the side opposite the yarns), fold it in half and make 1 overhand knot as close as possible to the ch.
Tighten the knot well, cut the yarns to a length of $^{6}/_{10}$in (1.5cm) and separate the strands for a "feather duster" effect.

BODY

In ecru. Crochet in the round, in closed rnds. The sl st that closes each rnd and the ch that starts each rnd are not indicated in the instructions, for better readability, but you must make them for each rnd. For more instructions, see the *Techniques* chapter, p. 22.
Rnd 1: 6 sc in a magic circle (6 st).
Rnd 2: 6 inc (12 st).
Rnd 3: (1 sc, 1 inc) x 6 (18 st).
Rnd 4: (1 sc, 1 inc, 1 sc) x 6 (24 st).
Rnd 5: BLO. In ecru: 20 sc; in brown; 2 sc; in ecru: 2 sc (24 st).
Rnd 6: 3 sc; in brown: 2 sc; in ecru: 16 sc; in brown: 1 sc; in ecru: 2 sc (24 st).
Rnd 7: 2 sc; in brown: 4 sc; in ecru: 18 sc (24 st).
Rnd 8: 2 sc; in brown: 2 sc; in ecru: 20 sc (24 st).
Rnd 9: 24 sc (24 st).
In brown, make and attach the back legs as explained in the instructions for the *Basic Shapes*, p. 28.
Rnd 10: (1 sc, 1 dec, 1 sc) x 6 (18 st).
Rnd 11: (1 sc, 1 dec) x 6 (12 st).
Cut the yarn, keeping a length of 4in (10cm).
Do not close yet.
Sew the tail at the back; insert the starting and ending yarns 1 st apart, tie them in a knot on the inside and cut them off.
With the pink yarn, embroider a small cross to represent a navel in the middle of the belly, straddling rnd 7.
In brown, make the front legs and attach them to the body as explained in the *Basic Shapes* section, p. 28. Then follow the rest of the instructions for that part to finish the cow.

Cat

 2 hours

 pp. 12, 13

Dimensions
Approximate height:
2⅓in (6cm)

Materials
› One 2.25mm crochet hook
› DMC Happy Cotton (¾oz–47yd [20g–43m]), shade 762, white 4/10oz (11g); shade 759, medium gray, 3¼yd (3m); shade 764, chamallow rose, 20in (50cm)
› DMC Lumina (¾oz–164yd [20g–150m]), shade L677, pink gold, 12in (30cm)
› Two 6mm (¼in) safety eyes
› Chenille stem, 2in (5cm) (optional)

EARS X 2

One ear in white and one ear in gray.
Crochet in a spiral.
Rnd 1: 4 sc in a magic circle (4 st).
Rnd 2: (1 inc, 1 sc) x 2 (6 st).
Rnd 3: (1 inc, 2 sc) x 2 (8 st).
Rnd 4: 1 sl st. Do not crochet the other st (8 st).
Cut the yarn to a length of 8in (20cm). Flatten the ear so that the yarn is at one end.
With the chamallow pink yarn and a needle, embroider 4 or 5 little lines 1 rnd in height to form a small triangle in the center of one face of each ear. I prefer to embroider them on the 3rd st of rnd 3 so that the ear is sewn facing the right direction.
Tie the yarns in a knot, cut them off, and pull the ends back into the ear.

HEAD

In white, follow the instructions for the Head given in *Basic Shapes*, p. 28.
After rnd 11, sew the ears on each side of the head, straddling rnds 3 to 5.
Tie the yarns in a knot on the inside and cut them off.
Finish crocheting the head.
With 8in (20cm) of gray yarn, embroider a small line of 2 or 3 thicknesses between rnds 10 and 11, between the eyes, to look like a muzzle.
If you wish, embroider or draw cheeks according to the instructions given in *Basic Shapes*, p. 28.
With the pink gold yarn, embroider two lines on each side of the head to be the whiskers, straddling rnds 10 and 11.

TAIL

In gray. Crochet in a spiral.
Rnd 1: 4 sc in a magic circle (4 st).
Rnd 2: 1 inc, 3 sc (5 st).
Rnd 3: 5 sc (5 st).
In white.
Rnds 4 to 7: 5 sc (5 st).
Rnd 8: 4 sc, 1 sl st (5 st).
Cut the yarn to a length of 8in (20cm).
Optional: To stiffen the tail, take a pipe cleaner and fold one end in, approximately half an inch down, with your fingers or pliers. Insert the pipe cleaner into the tail all the way until the end, and trim the excess, leaving ½in (1cm) remaining. Pull the pipe cleaner out slightly so you can fold over the remaining end, and insert it back into the tail.

BODY

Make the body in white, one hind leg in the same color and the other hind leg in gray. Make the front legs in white. Follow the instructions for the Body in *Basic Shapes*, p. 28.
Sew the tail at the back, straddling rnds 5 and 6 of the body. Tie the yarn in a knot on the inside and cut it off.

Pig

Dimensions

Approximate height: 2⅓in (6cm)

Materials

- One 2.25mm crochet hook
- DMC Happy Cotton (¾oz–47yd [20g–43m]), shade 763, layette pink, 60in (1.5m); shade 764, chamallow pink, ⁴⁄₁₀oz (11g)
- Two 6mm (¼in) safety eyes

EARS X 2

In chamallow pink.
Ch 5, keeping 4in (10cm) of starting yarn, 1 sc in the 2nd st away from the crochet hook; 2 hdc continuing along the ch; 1 sc at the end of the ch, ch 2, 1 sl st in the 2nd st away from the crochet hook, 1 sc again at the end of the ch; 2 hdc and 1 sc going up the other side of the ch.
Cut the yarn to a length of 6in (15cm). Using a needle, thread the starting yarn under the st to come out again at the base of the ear. Do not cut.

MUZZLE

In layette pink.
In a magic circle, make: 1 sc, 2 hdc, 2 sc, 2 hdc.
Cut the yarn to a length of 10in (25cm). Using a needle, thread this yarn under both loops of the first st made in the magic circle, from the front to the back. You now have a closed round with 8 st.
Keep the yarn for sewing the muzzle.

HEAD

In chamallow pink, follow the instructions for the Head in the *Basic Shapes* section, p. 28.
After rnd 11, sew the ears on each side of the head, straddling rnds 4 and 5.
Make a sewing st in the 1st and last st of the ear, and 1 additional st between them.
Bring the starting yarn to the inside of the head.
Tie a knot in the yarns on the inside without pulling too hard on the starting yarn so as not to distort the ear, and cut it off.
Finish crocheting the head.
Sew the muzzle between the eyes, straddling rnds 9 and 10. Position it so as to have the hdc on the sides, to have a slightly oval shape. Sew the BLO of the st of the muzzle.
If you wish, embroider or draw cheeks according to the instructions given in the *Basic Shapes* section, p. 28.

TAIL

In chamallow pink.
Ch 5, keeping 4in (10cm) of starting yarn, 1 sc in the 2nd st away from the crochet hook, 3 inc continuing along the ch.
Cut the yarn to a length of 4in (10cm).

BODY

In chamallow pink, follow the instructions for the Body in the *Basic Shapes* section, p. 28.
Once the body is finished, sew the tail to the back side, on the same rnd as the hind legs.
Pull the starting and ending yarns to the inside, 1 st apart, tie them together on the inside and cut them off.
With a layette pink yarn, embroider a little cross in the middle of the belly, straddling rnd 7, to resemble a navel.

Fox

Dimensions
Approximate height: 2¾in (7cm)

Materials
- One 2.25mm crochet hook
- DMC Happy Cotton (¾oz–47yd [20g–43m]), shade 753, tangerine orange, ⅓oz (10g); shade 775, black, 3¼yd (3m); shade 762, white, 7/100oz (2g)
- Two 6mm (¼in) safety eyes

EARS X 2

In black. Crochet in a spiral.
Rnd 1: 4 sc in a magic circle (4 st).
Rnd 2: (1 inc, 1 sc) x 2 (6 st).
In orange.
Rnd 3: (1 inc, 2 sc) x 2 (8 st).
Rnd 4: 1 inc, 7 sc (9 st).
Rnd 5: 1 sl st. Do not crochet the other st (9 st).
Cut the yarn to a length of 8in (20cm). Flatten the ears so that the yarn is at one end.

HEAD

In orange. Crochet in the round, in closed rnds.
The sl st that closes each rnd and the ch that starts each rnd are not indicated in the instructions, for better readability, but you must make then for each rnd. For more instructions, see the *Techniques* chapter, p. 22.
Rnd 1: 6 sc in a magic circle (6 st).
Rnd 2: 6 inc (12 st).
Rnd 3: (1 sc, 1 inc) x 6 (18 st).
Rnd 4: (1 sc, 1 inc, 1 sc) x 6 (24 st).
Rnd 5: (7 sc, 1 inc) x 3 (27 st).
Rnd 6: (3 sc, 1 inc, 5 sc) x 3 (30 st).
Rnds 7 to 10: 30 sc. Change color to white when making the last sc (30 st).
Rnd 11: (3 sc, 1 dec) x 6 (24 st).
Insert the safety eyes between rnds 9 and 10, in st 12 and 19 of rnd 9.
Sew the ears on each side of the head, straddling rnds 3 to 5. Tie the yarns in a knot on the inside and cut them off.
Start stuffing the head.
Rnd 12: (1 sc, 1 dec, 1 sc) x 6 (18 st).
Rnd 13: (1 dec, 1 sc) x 5, 1 dec, 1 sl st (12 st).
Cut the yarn, keeping a length of 12in (30cm) for sewing.
Finish stuffing the head.
With a black yarn, embroider the fox's muzzle as follows, making the line on top at the same level as the eyes:

If you wish, embroider or draw the cheeks according to the instructions given in the *Basic Shapes* section, p. 28.

TAIL

In white. Crochet in a spiral.
Rnd 1: 4 sc in a magic circle (4 st).
Rnd 2: (1 inc, 1 sc) x 2 (6 st).
In orange.
Rnd 3: (1 inc, 1 sc) x 3 (9 st).
Rnd 4: (1 inc, 2 sc) x 3 (12 st).
Rnd 5: (3 sc, 1 inc) x 3 (15 st).
Rnd 6: 15 sc (15 st).
Rnd 7: (3 sc, 1 dec) x 3 (12 st).
Start to stuff.
Rnd 8: (1 sc, 1 dec, 1 sc) x 3 (9 st).
Rnd 9: (1 dec, 1 sc) x 2, 1 dec, 1 sl st (6 st).
Cut the yarn to a length of 8in (20cm). Finish stuffing.

BODY

Make the body in orange and the legs in black, following the instructions for the Body in the *Basic Shapes* section, p. 28.
Sew the tail at the back, straddling rnds 5 and 6. Tie the yarn in a knot on the inside and cut it off.

Rabbit

1 hour 45 minutes

pp. 14, 15, and 17

Dimensions
Approximate height: 3¼in (8cm)

Materials
- One 2.25mm crochet hook
- DMC Happy Cotton (¾oz–47yd [20g–43m]), shade 762, white, ½oz (13g); shade 785, turquoise blue, 2¾yd (2.5m)
- DMC Lumina (¾oz–164yd [20g–150m]), shade L677, pink gold, 22yd (20m)
- "Fuzzy" yarn, white, 20in (50cm) (optional)
- Two 6mm (¼in) safety eyes

EARS X 2

In blue. Crochet in a spiral. Do not stuff.
Rnd 1: 6 sc in a magic circle (6 st).
Rnd 2: (1 inc, 1 sc) x 3 (9 st).
In white.
Rnds 3 to 7: 9 sc (9 st).
Rnd 8: (1 dec, 1 sc) x 3 (6 st).
Rnd 9: 1 sc, 1 sl st. Do not crochet the other st (6 st).
Cut the yarn to a length of 12in (30cm). Flatten the ears so that the yarn is at one end.

HEAD

In white, follow the instructions for the Head in the *Basic Shapes* section, p. 28.
After rnd 11, sew the ears on each side of the head, straddling rnds 3 and 4.
After having sewn around each ear, use the remaining yarn to make a few stitches through the ear, over half its height, to maintain the ear nice and flat at its base. Next, tie the yarn in a knot on the inside of the head and cut it off.
Finish crocheting the head. With a pink gold yarn, embroider a short line of several thicknesses to form the muzzle between rnds 10 and 11.
If you wish, embroider or draw the cheeks according to the instructions given in the *Basic Shapes* section, p. 28.

BODY

In white, follow the instructions for the Body in the *Basic Shapes* section, p. 28.
Take 20in (50cm) of white yarn (or of "fuzzy" white yarn, which will give the tail more of a "pompom" effect), and cut it in three pieces.
Using a needle, thread these three yarns through the back of the body: insert the needle in the 1st st of rnd 5, from the outside to the inside, and bring it out again through the last st of rnd 5. Tie the two ends of each yarn together, making a tight square knot, then cut the six yarns to a length of about ⅕in (5mm).
According to the type of yarn chosen, separate the strands of each yarn to give more volume.

Fawn

3 hours

pp. 14, 15, and 16

Dimensions
Approximate height: 2¾in (7cm)

Materials
- One 2.25mm crochet hook
- DMC Happy Cotton (¾oz–47yd [20g–43m]), shade 776, camel, ⅓oz (10g); shade 777, brown, 3¼yd (3m); shade 761, ecru, 1/7oz (4g)
- DMC Pearl Cotton Size 5, shade 310, black, 16in (40cm)
- Two 6mm (¼in) safety eyes

A brilliant fawn can be made with a 2.5mm crochet hook, and by replacing the camel color with two thicknesses of DMC Lumina (¾oz–164yd [20g–150 m]), shade L677, pink gold, and two thicknesses of DMC Diamant metallic embroidery thread, shade D301 (a single thickness for the ears), that is four thicknesses crocheted simultaneously (three for the ears).

EARS X 2

In camel. Crochet in a spiral.
Rnd 1: 4 sc in a magic circle (4 st).
Rnd 2: (1 inc, 1 sc) x 2 (6 st).
Rnd 3: (1 inc, 1 sc) x 3 (9 st).
Rnd 4: 1 inc, 8 sc (10 st).
Rnd 5: 1 dec, 8 sc (9 st).
Rnd 6: (1 sc, 1 dec) x 3 (6 st).
Rnd 7: 1 sl st. Do not crochet the other st (6 st).
Cut the yarn to a length of 8in (20cm). Flatten the ear so that the yarn is at one end.
With the ecru yarn, embroider 2 small vertical lines, 2 rnds high, in the middle of each ear.
I prefer to embroider them on the side of the 2nd and 3rd st of rnd 6 so that the ear is sewn in the right direction. Tie the yarns in a knot, cut them off, and pull them inside the ear.

HORNS X 2

In brown. Crochet in a spiral.
Rnd 1: 4 sc in a magic circle (4 st).
Rnd 2: 1 inc, 3 sc (5 st).
Rnd 3: 1 sl st. Do not crochet the other st (5 st).
Cut the yarn to a length of 8in (20cm). Add a little stuffing to each horn.

MUZZLE

In ecru. Crochet in a spiral.
Rnd 1: 4 sc in a magic circle (4 st).
Rnd 2: 2 inc, 1 sl st. Do not crochet the last st (6 st).
Cut the yarn to a length of 8in (20cm).
With the 8in (20cm) length of brown yarn, embroider a little nose at the top of the muzzle, over the 3rd and 4th st of rnd 1, then a little vertical line starting from the point of the nose. Tie the two brown yarns in a knot and cut them off.

HEAD

In camel. Crochet in a spiral.
Rnd 1: 6 sc in a magic circle (6 st).
Rnd 2: 6 inc (12 st).
Rnd 3: (1 sc, 1 inc) x 6 (18 st).
Rnd 4: 1 sc, 1 inc, 1 sc) x 6 (24 st).
Rnd 5: (7 sc, 1 inc) x 3 (27 st).
Rnd 6: (3 sc, 1 inc, 5 sc) x 3 (30 st).
Rnd 7: 9 sc; in ecru: 4 sc; in camel: 3 sc; in ecru: 4 sc; in camel: 10 sc (30 st).
Rnds 8 and 9: 8 sc; in ecru: 6 sc; in camel: 1 sc; in ecru: 6 sc; in camel: 9 sc (30 st).
Rnd 10: 8 sc; in ecru: 13 sc; in camel: 9 sc (30 st).
Rnd 11: 1 sc, 1 dec, 3 sc, 1 dec, 1 sc; in ecru: (2 sc, 1 dec, 1 sc) x 2, 2 sc; in camel: 1 dec, 3 sc, 1 dec, 2 sc (24 st).

After rnd 11, insert the safety eyes between rnds 9 and 10, in st 12 and 19 of rnd 9.
Before attaching the washers on the back, embroider two small lines in black Pearl Cotton, at the outside of each eye. Each black eyelash starts from the st where the safety eye is inserted and runs diagonally, 1 st toward the exterior and 1 rnd upward.
Attach the washers to the back of the eyes.
Sew the ears on each side of the head, straddling rnds 5 and 6. Tie the yarns on the inside and cut them off.
Sew the horns over rnd 3 of the head, between the ears. Tie the yarns and cut them off.
Start to stuff the head.
Rnd 12: (1 sc, 1 dec, 1 sc) x 2; in ecru: (1 sc, 1 dec, 1 sc) x 2; in camel: (1 sc, 1 dec, 1 sc) x 2 (18 st).
Rnd 13: (1 dec, 1 sc) x 2; in ecru: (1 dec, 1 sc) x 2; in camel: (1 dec, 1 sc) x 2 (12 st).
Cut the yarn to a length of 12in (30cm).
Finish stuffing the head. Sew the muzzle by placing it between the eyes, straddling rnds 10 to 12 of the head.
With 20in (50cm) of ecru yarn and a needle, embroider three little Vs on the front of the head, between the ears, on rnds 4 and 6 as shown:

Then embroider five more Vs at the back of the head, on rnds 5, 7, 8, and 10, following the diagram below:

If you wish, embroider or draw the cheeks according to the instructions given in the *Basic Shapes* section, p. 28.

BELLY

In ecru. Crochet in rows.
Row 1: Ch 5, keeping 4in (10cm) of starting yarn, 1 sc in the 2nd st away from the crochet hook, 3 sc continuing along the ch. Turn the work (4 st).
Rows 2 to 4: Ch 1, 4 sc. Turn (4 st).
Row 5: Ch 1, 1 sc, flow 2 st together, 1 sc (3 st).
Ch 1 to stop the piece. Cut the yarn to a length of 15in (40cm).

TAIL

In camel.
Ch 3, keeping 6in (15cm) of starting yarn, 1 sl st in the 2nd st away from the crochet hook, 1 sc in the next st.
Cut the yarn to a length of 4in (10cm).

BODY

Make the body in camel and the legs in brown.
Follow the instructions for the Body in the *Basic Shapes* section, p. 28.
Sew the belly by placing the starting ch between the hind legs, on the same rnd.
The belly is placed across rnds 5 to 10 of the body.
Sew all around, then tie the yarn in a knot on the inside and cut it off.
Sew the tail to the back side. Insert the starting and ending yarns of the tail through the body, 1 st apart. Tie them in a knot on the inside and cut them off.
With 12in (30cm) of ecru yarn and a needle, embroider five small Vs on the back of the body, over rnds 6, 7, and 9, following the diagram below:

Squirrel

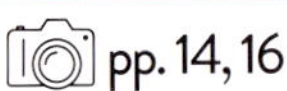

Dimensions
Approximate height: 2⅓in (6cm)

Materials

- One 2.25mm crochet hook
- DMC Happy Cotton (¾oz–47yd [20g–43m]), shade 776, camel, ⅓oz (9g); shade 761, ecru, 2¼yd (2m); shade 777, brown, 1/7oz (4g)
- DMC Lumina (¾oz–164yd [20g–150m]), shade L677, pink gold, 1/7oz (4g). Divide this length into three equal parts. Crochet the parts in pink gold by using these three yarns simultaneously, to have a thickness similar to that of Happy Cotton (optional, replacing brown Happy Cotton).
- Two 6mm (¼in) safety eyes

EARS X 2

In camel.
In a magic circle, make: ch 1, 1 hdc, 7 sc, 2 hdc. After tightening the circle, do not cut the remaining starting yarn. Fold the small circle obtained in half, placing the 1st hdc over the next-to-last one. Crochet simultaneously in both thicknesses: insert the crochet hook in the BL of the 1st hdc and in the BL of the next-to-last hdc (skip the last hdc), and make 1 sl st. Make 3 more sl st in the same manner.
The starting yarn of the magic circle should come out beside the last sl st.
Cut the ending yarn to a length of 8in (20cm). Using a needle, bring this yarn to the inside of the ear and bring it back out again at the bottom of the ear, beside the hdc st.

HEAD

In camel. Crochet in a spiral.
Rnd 1: 6 sc in a magic circle (6 st).
Rnd 2: 6 inc (12 st).
Rnd 3: (1 sc, 1 inc) x 6 (18 st).
Rnd 4: (1 sc, 1 inc, 1 sc) x 6 (24 st).
Rnd 5: (7 sc, 1 inc) x 3 (27 st).
Rnd 6: (3 sc, 1 inc, 5 sc) x 3 (30 st).
Rnds 7 to 10: 30 sc (30 st).
Rnd 11: (3 sc, 1 dec) x 2, 3 sc; in ecru: 1 dec, 2 sc; in camel: 1 sc, 1 dec, (3 sc, 1 dec) x 2 (24 st).
Insert the safety eyes between rnds 9 and 10, in st 12 and 19 of rnd 9.
Sew the ears to the head, above and slightly behind the eyes, on rnd 4. Make 2 sewing stitches above and below this rnd so that the ears are securely held in place. Tie the yarn in a knot on the inside and cut it off. Cut the starting yarn that extends from the ears to a scant half inch and separate the strands to give a fuzzy effect to the ears.
Start to stuff the head.
Rnd 12: (1 sc, 1 dec, 1 sc) x 2, 1 sc, 1 dec; in ecru: 3 sc; in camel: 1 dec, (1 sc, 1 dec, 1 sc) x 2 (18 st).
Rnd 13: (1 dec, 1 sc) x 5, 1 dec, 1 sl st (12 st).
Cut the yarn to a length of 12in (30cm).
Finish stuffing the head. With a brown yarn (or pink gold), embroider a small line of several thicknesses just above the white part of the head, between the eyes. If you wish, embroider or draw the cheeks according to the instructions given in the *Basic Shapes* section, p. 28.

TAIL

In brown (or pink gold). Crochet in a spiral.
Stuff very lightly as you go along, so you will be able to roll up the end of the tail.

Rnd 1: Ch 6, 1 sc in the 2nd st away from the crochet hook; 3 sc continuing along the ch; 3 sc in the st at the end of the ch; 3 sc and 1 inc going back up the other side of the ch (12 st).
Rnds 2 to 19: 12 sc (12 st).
Do not stuff any more before closing.
Rnd 20: 2 sc, 1 sl st. Next, crochet the two thicknesses edge to edge; insert the crochet hook in the next st and then in the 1st st of rnd 20, and make 1 sc; make 3 sc more and 1 sl st.
Cut the yarn to a length of 20in (50cm).
To roll the tail: Fold the top so as to place the st of the last rnd of the tail at the level of the 12th rnd. Make several stitches across the width of the tail. Continue gently rolling the tail, and make a 2nd line of stitching 3 rnds lower to maintain the tail position. Bring the yarn inside the tail and bring it out again at the bottom, then make an unobtrusive knot. You will use this yarn to sew the tail to the body.

BELLY

In ecru. Crochet in a spiral.
Rnd 1: 6 sc in a magic circle (6 st).
Rnd 2: 6 inc (12 st).
Rnd 3: 1 sl st. Do not crochet the other st (12 st).
Cut the yarn to a length of 10in (25cm).

BODY

In camel. Follow the instructions for the Body in the *Basic Shapes* section, p. 28.
Sew the belly between the legs, straddling rnds 6 to 10. Tie the yarn in a knot on the inside and cut it off.
Sew the base of the tail to the back of the body, straddling rnds 5 to 8. Make sewing stitches all around, in a square, to hold it well.
Tie the yarn in a knot on the inside and cut it off.

Owl

2 hours

pp. 14, 17

Dimensions
Approximate height: 3in (7.5cm)

Materials
- One 2.25mm crochet hook
- DMC Happy Cotton (¾oz–47 yd [20g–43m]), shade 782, almond green, ⅓oz (9g); shade 762, white, 3¼yd (3m); shade 788, lemon yellow, 20in (50cm)
- DMC Lumina (¾oz–164yd [20g–150m]), shade L3821, gold, 6in (15m). Divide this length into three equal parts. Crochet the parts in pink gold by using these three yarns simultaneously, to have a thickness similar to that of Happy Cotton.
- Two 6mm (¼in) safety eyes

EARS X 2

In almond green. Crochet in a spiral.
Rnd 1: 4 sc in a magic circle (4 st).
Rnd 2: (1 inc, 1 sc) x 2 (6 st).
Rnd 3: 1 sl st. Do not crochet the other st (6 st).
Cut the yarn to a length of 8in (20cm).

BEAK

In yellow.
Ch 4, keeping 4in (10cm) of starting yarn, 1 sc in the 2nd st away from the crochet hook, 1 hdc in the following st and 1 dc in the last st.
Cut the yarn to a length of 6in (15cm).

WINGS X 2

In gold. Crochet in a spiral.
Rnd 1: 6 sc in a magic circle (6 st).
Rnd 2: 6 inc (12 st).
Rnd 3: (1 sc, 1 inc) x 6 (18 st).
Rnd 4: 1 sl st. Do not crochet the other st (18 st).
Cut the yarn to a length of 10in (25cm). Bring the starting yarn under a few st and cut it off flush with the surface.

BODY

In almond green. Crochet in a spiral.
Rnd 1: 6 sc in a magic circle (6 st).
Rnd 2: 6 inc (12 st).
Rnd 3: (1 sc, 1 inc) x 6 (18 st).
Rnd 4: (1 sc, 1 inc, 1 sc) x 6 (24 st).
Rnd 5: (7 sc, 1 inc) x 3 (27 st).
Rnd 6: 3 sc, 1 inc, 5 sc; in white: 3 sc; in almond green: 1 inc, 2 sc; in white: 3 sc; in almond green: 3 sc, 1 inc, 5 sc (30 st).
Rnd 7: 9 sc; in white: 5 sc; in almond green: 2 sc; in white: 5 sc; in almond green: 8 sc (30 st).
Rnd 8: 9 sc; in white: 5 sc; in almond green: 2 sc; in white: 6 sc; in almond green: 8 sc (30 sc).
Rnds 9 and 10: 9 sc; in white: 13 sc; in almond green: 8 sc (30 st).
Rnd 11: 30 sc (30 st).
Rnd 12: (1 inc, 9 sc) x 3 (33 st).
Insert the safety eyes between rnds 8 and 9, in st 12 and 20 of rnd 8.
Sew the ears straddling rnds 4 and 5 of the head. The bottom of each ear must be positioned with 1 st between the ear and the white part of the head.
Tie the yarns in a knot on the inside and cut them off.
Sew the beak on flat, positioning the hdc at the top, horizontally. It must be positioned between the eyes, straddling rnds 9 and 10.
Tie the yarns in a knot on the inside and cut them off.
Rnds 13 to 17: 33 sc (33 st).
Rnd 18: (1 dec, 9 sc) x 3 (30 st).
Start stuffing the body.
Rnd 19: (1 sc, 1 dec) x 10 (20 st).
Rnd 20: 10 dec (10 st).
Rnd 21: 5 dec (5 st).
Close.
Sew the wings on each side of the body, at the lower corners of the white part. Make 2 sewing stitches on this line, then 2 additional stitches along a vertical line of each side of the wing to give the wing a curved shape.
With 24in (60cm) of gold yarn, embroider five Vs on the body to look like feathers, on rnds 13 and 15.
If you wish, embroider or draw the cheeks according to the instructions given in the *Basic Shapes* section, p. 28.

Octopus

 1 hour 30 minutes

 pp. 18, 19

Dimensions
Approximate height:
2¾in (7cm)

Preliminary information
The two parts of the body are crocheted in the round, in closed rnds. The sl st that closes each rnd and the ch that starts each rnd are not indicated in the directions, for better readability, **but you must make them for each rnd.** For more instructions, see the *Techniques* chapter, p. 22.
A larger version of this mini-octopus is available in the book, Adorable Animals, *which is part of the same collection.*

Materials
- One 2.25mm crochet hook
- DMC Happy Cotton (¾oz–47yd [20g–43m]), **for the blue design:** shade 785, turquoise blue, ⅓oz (9g); shade 762, white, 5½yd (5m); **for the pink design:** shade 764, chamallow pink, ⅓oz (9g)
- DMC Lumina (¾oz–164yd [20g–150m]), shade L3821, gold, 16yd (15m).
  Divide this length into three equal parts. Crochet the parts in gold by using these three yarns simultaneously, to have a thickness similar to that of Happy Cotton (for the pink design only).
- DMC Pearl Cotton Size 5, shade 310, black, 8in (20cm)
- Two 6mm (¼in) safety eyes

BODY, 1st PART

In blue (or pink).
Rnd 1: 6 sc in a magic circle (6 st).
Rnd 2: 6 inc (12 st).
Rnd 3: (1 sc, 1 inc) x 6 (18 st).
Rnd 4: (1 sc, 1 inc, 1 sc) x 6 (24 st).
Rnd 5: (7 sc, 1 inc) x 3 (27 st).
Rnd 6: (3 sc, 1 inc, 5 sc) x 3 (30 st).
Rnds 7 to 10: 30 sc (30 st).
Rnd 11: (3 sc, 1 dec) x 6 (24 st).
Insert the safety eyes between rnds 8 and 9, in st 12 and 19 of rnd 8.
Rnd 12: (1 sc, 1 dec) x 8 (16 st).
In white (or gold).
Rnd 13: [Ch 8 rather loosely, 1 sl st in the 2nd st away from the crochet hook; continuing along the ch: 2 sc, 4 hdc; skip the next st on rnd 12 and make 1 sl st in the following st on rnd 12 and make 1 sl st in the next st to attach the tentacle to the body] x 8, to make 8 tentacles.
Cut the yarn and stop it by bringing the starting yarn to the inside at the place where the 1st tentacle starts. Make a knot on the inside of the octopus body.
Stuff the body.

BODY, 2nd PART

In blue (or pink).
Rnd 1: 8 sc in a magic circle (8 st).
Rnd 2: 8 inc (16 st).
Rnd 3: [Ch 8 rather loosely, 1 sl st in the 2nd st away from the crochet hook; continuing along the ch: 2 sc, 4 hdc; skip the next st on rnd 2 and make 1 sl st in the following st to attach the tentacle to the body] x 8, to make 8 tentacles.
Do not cut the yarn, it will be used for the assembly.

ASSEMBLY

Crochet the two parts together to assemble them, making sl st all around the edges of the 8 tentacles. (Make the sl st rather tight to obtain tentacles that are curved a bit upward.) Position the two parts back to back, placing the 1st tentacle of the 2nd part back to back with the last tentacle of the 1st part. Pin each tentacle to its corresponding tentacle on the other part to hold each in place. Starting from the end of the 2nd part of the body, after the last sl st made:

Make 1 sl st, then turn the work so as to insert the crochet hook first into the top tentacle (the white or gold one). Insert the crochet hook in the 1st st of the top tentacle (the 1st sl st made in rnd 13 of the 1st part, the one in which you made the last hdc of the tentacle), then in both loops of the last hdc of the bottom tentacle (the blue or pink one), and make 1 sl st.

Repeat this 6 more times in all the st, advancing along the edge of the tentacle, up to the point. To easily locate where to insert the crochet hook in the top tentacle, look on the starting ch for the place where you inserted the crochet hook to make the st that formed the tentacle (as a reminder: 4 hdc, 2 sc, 1 sl st). By pulling a little to spread out the st, you will see a hole at that point. In the bottom tentacle, all you have to do is insert the crochet hook in both loops of each st.

Work your way back down the other edge of the tentacles, making 7 sl st as well. In the top tentacle, insert the crochet hook in both loops of the st, and in the bottom tentacle, insert the crochet hook in the starting ch.

Finish the tentacle by making 1 last sl st: insert the crochet hook in the same st as those in which you made the sl st to attach the tentacles. Then insert the crochet hook in rnd 12 of the 1st part of the body, and in rnd 2 of the 2nd part.

Repeat all these steps for 5 more tentacles. Finish stuffing the body, then crochet the last two tentacles together.

Cut the yarn to a length of 10in (25cm). Tighten the last sl st well, pull the yarn to the inside, making several round trips in the stuffing, and cut it off flush with the surface.

With the black Pearl Cotton, embroider a little smile in the form of a V, straddling rnd 10, between the eyes.

If you wish, embroider or draw the cheeks according to the instructions given in the *Basic Shapes* section, p. 28.

Penguin

2 hours 45 minutes

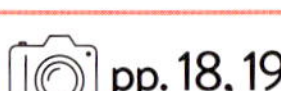
pp. 18, 19

Dimensions

Approximate height: 2⅓in (6cm)

Materials

- One 2.25mm crochet hook
- DMC Happy Cotton (¾oz–47yd [20g–43m]), shade 758, navy blue, ⅓oz (9g); shade 762, white, 1/10oz (3g); shade 788, lemon yellow, 39in (1m)
- Two 6mm (¼in) safety eyes

BEAK

In yellow. Crochet in a spiral.

Rnd 1: 5 sc in a magic circle (5 st).

Rnd 2: (1 inc, 1 sc) x 2, 1 inc (8 st).

Rnd 3: 1 sl st. Do not crochet the other st (8 st).

Cut the yarn to a length of 8in (20cm).

HEAD

In blue. Crochet in a spiral.

Rnd 1: 6 sc in a magic circle (6 st).
Rnd 2: 6 inc (12 st).
Rnd 3: (1 sc, 1 inc) x 6 (18 st).
Rnd 4: (1 sc, 1 inc, 1 sc) x 6 (24 st).
Rnd 5: (7 sc, 1 inc) x 3 (27 st).
Rnd 6: (3 sc, 1 inc, 5 sc) x 3 (30 st).
Rnd 7: 8 sc; in white: 5 sc; in blue: 2 sc; in white: 5 sc; in blue: 10 sc (30 st).
Rnds 8 and 9: 8 sc; in white: 6 sc; in blue: 1 sc; in white: 6 sc; in blue: 9 sc (30 st).
Rnd 10: 8 sc; in white: 13 sc; in blue: 9 sc (30 st).
Rnd 11: 1 sc, 1 dec, 3 sc, 1 dec, 1 sc; in white: (2 sc, 1 dec, 1 sc) x 2, 2 sc; in blue: 1 dec, 3 sc, 1 dec, 2 sc (24 st).
Insert the safety eyes between rnds 9 and 10, in st 12 and 19 of rnd 9.
Start stuffing the head.
Rnd 12: (1 sc, 1 dec, 1 sc) x 2; in white: (1 sc, 1 dec, 1 sc) x 2, 1 sc; in blue: 1 dec, 2 sc, 1 dec, 1 sc (18 st).
Rnd 13: (1 dec, 1 sc) x 2, in white: (1 dec, 1 sc) x 2; in blue: (1 dec, 1 sc) x 2 (12 st).
Cut the yarn to a length of 12in (30cm).
Finish stuffing the head. Place the beak between the eyes, straddling rnds 10 to 12 of the head, and sew it there.
If you wish, embroider or draw the cheeks according to the instructions given in the *Basic Shapes* section, p. 28.

WINGS X 2

In blue.
Ch 7, keeping 4in (10cm) of starting yarn: 1 sl st in the 2nd st away from the crochet hook; continuing along the ch: 1 sc, 1 hdc, 1 dc, 2 tr.
Cut the yarn to a length of 8in (20cm).

TAIL

In blue.
In a magic circle, keeping 4in (10cm) of starting yarn, make: 1 sc, 2 hdc, 1 sc.
Cut the yarn to a length of 6in (15cm).

BODY

In blue. Crochet in the round, in closed rnds.
The sl st that closes each rnd and the ch that starts each rnd are not indicated in the instructions, for better readability, but you must make them for each rnd. For more instructions, see the *Techniques* chapter, p. 22.

Rnd 1: 6 sc in a magic circle (6 st).
Rnd 2: 6 inc (12 st).
Rnd 3: (1 sc, 1 inc) x 6 (18 st).
Rnd 4: (1 sc, 1 inc, 1 sc) x 6 (24 st).
Rnd 5: Crochet the entire rnd in BLO: 9 sc; in white: 6 sc; in blue: 9 sc (24 st).
Rnds 6 to 9: 9 sc; in white: 6 sc; in blue: 9 sc (24 st).
In yellow, make and attach the hind legs to the body as explained in the instructions for the Body in *Basic Shapes*, p. 28.
Rnd 10: (1 sc, 1 dec, 1 sc) x 2, 1 sc; in white: 1 dec, 2 sc, 1 dec; in blue: 1 sc, (1 sc, 1 dec, 1 sc) x 2 (18 st).
Rnd 11: 1 dec, 1 sc, 2 dec; in white; 4 sc; in blue: 2 dec, 1 sc, 1 dec (12 st).
With the ending yarn, sew the 1st and last st of the tail to the back of the body, leaving 1 st of space between the stitches. Tie the starting and ending yarns on the inside of the body and cut them off.
Sew the wings on each side of the body.
Pull one of the yarns of the wing through a st at the edge of the white part of the body, between rnds 9 and 10. Pull the other yarn through a st 3 st further back, between rnds 11 and 12 of the body.
Make a few sewing stitches along the upper part of the wings and leave the bottom free. Pull the yarns to the inside, tie them in a knot, and cut them off.
To finish the penguin, follow the instructions for Assembly in *Basic Shapes*, p. 29.

Whale

Dimensions
Approximate length:
2¾in (7cm)

Materials
› One 2.25mm crochet hook
› DMC Happy Cotton (¾oz–47yd [20g–43m]), shade 785, turquoise ⅓oz (9g); shade 762, white, ⅐oz (4g)
› DMC Pearl Cotton Size 5, shade 310, black, 12in (30cm)
› Two 6mm x 8mm (¼in x ⅓in) safety eyes

FINS X 2

In turquoise.
In a magic circle, keeping 4in (10cm) of starting yarn, make: ch 1, 1 hdc, 4 dc, 1 hdc, 1 sl st.
Cut the yarn to a length of 6in (15cm).

SPOUT

In white. Crochet in a spiral.
Rnd 1: 6 sc in a magic circle (6 st).
Rnd 2: 6 sc in the BLO (6 st).
Rnd 3: 1 sc in both loops, then in the FLO: (1 sc, 2 hdc, 1 sc) in 1 st x 5 (21 st).
Rnd 4: In the FLO: 1 sc and 2 hdc in 1 st. Do not crochet the other st (23 st).
Cut the yarn to a length of 6in (15cm). Stop the yarn invisibly and pull the yarn to the inside, bringing it out again at the base of the spout

BELLY

In white. Crochet in a spiral.
Rnd 1: 6 sc in a magic circle (6 st).
Rnd 2: 6 inc (12 st).
Rnd 3: 1 sc, 3 inc, 3 sc, 3 inc, 2 sc (18 st).
Rnd 4: (1 sc, 1 inc) x 3, 3 sc, (1 sc, 1 inc) x 3, 3 sc (24 st).
Rnd 5: 2 sc, (1 sc, 1 inc) x 3, 6 sc, (1 sc, 1 inc) x 3, 4 sc (30 st).
Rnd 6: 3 sc, (3 inc, 1 sc) x 2, 7 sc, (3 inc, 1 sc) x 2, 3 sc, 1 sl st (42 st).
Cut the yarn to a length of 4in (10cm). Stop it invisibly and tie the yarn in a knot on the back side.
Mark the BL of st 10 of rnd 6.

TAIL

In turquoise. Crochet in a spiral.
1st part
Rnd 1: 6 sc in a magic circle (6 st).
Rnd 2: (1 inc, 1 sc) x 3 (9 st).
Rnd 3: 8 sc, 1 sl st (9 st).
Cut the yarn and stop it invisibly, without closing this part.
2nd part
Rnds 1 to 3: Repeat rnds 1 to 3 of the 1st part.
Rnd 4: Attach the two parts together by making 1 sl st in one st of rnd 3 of the 1st part; 1 sc in the next st (this st becomes the 1st st of the rnd), 1 sc, 2 dec, 2 sc; continue by inserting the crochet hook in the 2nd part of the tail 1 sc in the 1st st of rnd 3, 1 sc, 2 dec, 2 sc (12 st).
Start stuffing.
Rnd 5: 1 sc, 2 dec, 2 sc, 2 dec, 1 sl st (8 st).
Finish stuffing. Cut the yarn to a length of 10in (25cm).

BODY

In turquoise. Crochet in a spiral.
Rnd 1: 6 sc in a magic circle (6 st).
Rnd 2: 6 inc (12 st).
Rnd 3: (1 sc, 1 inc) x 6 (18 st).
Rnd 4: (1 sc, 1 inc, 1 sc) x 6 (24 st).
Rnd 5: (1 inc, 3 sc) x 6 (30 st).
Rnd 6: 1 inc, (3 sc, 1 inc, 3 sc) x 4, 1 inc (36 st).
Rnd 7: 36 sc (36 st).
Rnd 8: 2 sc, 1 inc, 30 sc, 1 inc, 2 sc (38 st).
Rnd 9: 38 sc (38 st).
Rnd 10: 1 inc, 36 sc, 1 inc (40 st).
Rnd 11: 40 sc (40 st).
Rnd 12: 2 sc, 1 inc, 34 sc, 1 inc, 2 sc (42 st).
Rnd 13: 42 sc (42 st).
Cut the yarn to a length of 16in (40cm).
Insert the safety eyes between rnds 11 and 12, in st 12 and 27 of rnd 11.

ASSEMBLY

Sew the spout to the top of the body:
insert the crochet hook in the FL of the 1st rnd of the spout and in all 6 st of rnd 1 of the body. Bring the starting yarn to the inside, tie the two yarns together on the inside of the body, and cut them off.
Sew the fins over rnd 13 of the body, 1 st behind each eye. Make a sewing stitch in the 1st st and in the last st of each fin. Bring the starting yarn to the inside. Tie the starting and ending yarns together on the inside and cut them off.
With the ending yarn of the body, sew the body and the belly together: insert the needle in the BL of the previously marked st on the belly, from the front to the back, then in both loops of the 1st st of rnd 13 of the body, from the inside to the outside. Sew like that for three-quarters of the length, always inserting the needle in the BL of the st of the belly and in both loops of the st of the body. Stuff the body.
Continue sewing, adding a little stuffing, if necessary, before making the last sewing stitches.
Sew the tail to the back of the body, centered between the two eyes, straddling rnd 13 of the body and the seam that joins the belly and the body.
With the black Pearl Cotton, embroider a line to represent a smile, between the eyes, on the seam between the belly and the body. I embroider a rather wide smile, starting at about 2 st inside one eye and stopping at about 2 st inside the other eye.
If you wish, embroider or draw cheeks according to the instructions given in the *Basic Shapes* section, p. 28.

Shark

Dimensions
Approximate length: 3⅛in (8cm)

Materials
› One 2.25mm crochet hook
› DMC Happy Cotton (¾oz–47yd [20g–43m]), shade 759, medium gray, 3/100oz (8g); shade 762, white, 7/100oz (2g)
› DMC Pearl Cotton Size 5, shade 310, black, 12in (30cm)
› Two 4.5mm (1/5in) safety eyes

LATERAL FINS X 2

In gray. Crochet in a spiral.
Rnd 1: 4 sc in a magic circle (4 st).
Rnd 2: (1 inc, 1 sc) x 2 (6 st).
Rnd 3: 1 sc, 1 inc, 2 sc, 1 inc, 1 sl st (8 st).
Cut the yarn to a length of 8in (20cm). Flatten the fins.

DORSAL FIN

In gray. Crochet in a spiral.
Rnd 1: 4 sc in a magic circle (4 st).
Rnd 2: (1 inc, 1 sc) x 2 (6 st).
Rnd 3: (1 inc, 1 sc) x 3 (9 st).
Rnd 4: (1 sc, 1 inc, 1 sc) x 2, 1 sc, 1 inc, 1 sl st (12 st).
Cut the yarn to a length of 10in (25cm). Flatten the fin.

TAIL

In gray. Crochet in a spiral.
1st part
Rnd 1: 4 sc in a magic circle (4 st).
Rnd 2: (1 inc, 1 sc) x 2 (6 st).
Rnd 3: (1 sc, 1 inc, 1 sc) x 2 (8 st).
Rnd 4: 7 sc, 1 sl st (8 st).
Cut the yarn and stop it invisibly, without closing this part.
2nd part
Rnds 1 and 2: Repeat rnds 1 and 2 from the 1st part.
Rnd 3: 1 sc, 1 inc, 2 sc, 1 inc, 1 sl st (8 st).
Rnd 4: Crochet the 2 parts together by making 1 sl st in a st of rnd 4 of the 1st part; 1 sc in the following st (this sc becomes the 1st st of the rnd), 6 sc; continue by inserting the needle in the 2nd part of the tail 1 sc in the 1st st of rnd 3, 6 sc (14 st).
Cut the yarn to a length of 12in (30cm). Flatten the tail.

BODY

In gray. Crochet in a spiral.
Rnd 1: Ch 6, 1 sc in the 2nd st away from the crochet hook; 3 sc continuing along the ch; 3 sc in the st at the end of the ch; 3 sc and 1 inc coming back up the other side of the ch (12 st).
Rnd 2: 1 inc, 3 sc, 3 inc, 3 sc, 2 inc (18 st).
Rnd 3: 1 inc, 6 sc, 3 inc, 6 sc, 2 inc (24 st).
Rnd 4: 4 sc, 1 inc, 4 sc, (1 inc, 1 sc) x 2, 3 sc, 1 inc, 3 sc, (1 sc, 1 inc) x 2 (30 st).
Rnd 5: 11 sc, 3 inc, 12 sc, 3 inc, 1 sc (36 st).
Rnd 6: 5 sc, 1 inc, 7 sc, (1 inc, 1 sc) x 2, 6 sc, 1 inc, 7 sc, (1 inc, 1 sc) x 2, 1 sc (42 st).
Rnd 7: 15 sc, (1 inc, 1 sc) x 2, 17 sc, (1 inc, 1 sc) x 2, 2 sc (46 st).
Rnd 8: 46 sc (46 st).
Rnd 9: 16 sc, 2 dec, 19 sc, 2 dec, 2 sc, 1 sl st (42 st).
Cut the yarn to a length of 4in (10cm). Stop it invisibly.

In white.

Rnd 10: Pull a yarn through the false st that you created when stopping the gray yarn. Make 1 ch and 1 sc in the same st. Mark this sc as the 1st st of the rnd, 13 sc, 3 dec, 15 sc, 3 dec, 1 sc (36 st).

Rnd 11: (12 sc, 3 dec) x 2 (30 st).

Rnd 12: (3 sc, 1 dec) x 6 (24 st).

Insert the safety eyes between rnds 8 and 9, in st 12 and 24 of rnd 8.

Sew on the fins and tail before continuing to crochet. Sew the dorsal fin to the top of the body, around the 12 st of rnd 1.

Sew the lateral fins on each side of the body, over rnd 10, 3 st to the outside of each eye.

Sew the tail on vertically at the back of the body, straddling rnds 7 to 9, positioning the larger half of the tail at the top.

Bring the various yarns to the inside, tie them in knots, and cut them off.

Start stuffing the body.

Rnd 13: (1 sc, 1 dec, 1 sc) x 6 (18 st).

Rnd 14: (1 sc, 1 dec) x 6 (12 st).

Finish stuffing.

Rnd 15: 6 dec (6 st).

Close.

With black Pearl Cotton, embroider a zigzag line to resemble teeth between the eyes, straddling rnd 10.

If you wish, embroider or draw the cheeks according to the instructions given in the *Basic Shapes* section, p. 28.

Turtle

2 hours

pp. 18, 19

Dimensions

Approximate length: 3¼in (8.5cm)

Materials

- One 2.5mm crochet hook
- DMC Happy Cotton (¾oz–47yd [20g–43m]), shade 781, malachite green, 1/10oz (3g); shade 783, water green, ⅓oz (9g)
- DMC Pearl Cotton Size 5, shade 310, black, 12in (30cm)
- Two 5mm (1/5in) safety eyes

HEAD

In malachite green. Crochet in a spiral.
Rnd 1: 6 sc in a magic circle (6 st).
Rnd 2: 6 inc (12 st).
Rnd 3: (1 sc, 1 inc) x 6 (18 st).
Rnd 4: (4 sc, 1 inc, 1 sc) x 3 (21 st).
Rnds 5 to 8: 21 sc (21 st).
Place the eyes between rnds 6 and 7, in st 6 and 16 of rnd 6.
Rnd 9: (4 sc, 1 dec, 1 sc) x 3 (18 st).
Start stuffing the head.
Rnd 10: (1 sc, 1 dec) x 6 (12 st).
Rnd 11: (1 dec, 1 sc) x 4 (8 st).
Finish stuffing.
Rnd 12: 8 sc (8 st).
Rnd 13: 2 sc, 1 sl st. Do not crochet the other st (8 st).
Cut the yarn and keep 10in (25cm) for sewing.

LARGE FINS X 2

In malachite green. Crochet in a spiral.
Rnd 1: 9 sc in a magic circle, well tightened (9 st).
Rnd 2: 9 inc (18 st).
Rnd 3: (1 inc, 1 sc) x 8, 1 inc, 1 sl st (27 st).
Fold the round piece you just made in half.
Continue crocheting the two thicknesses simultaneously.
Rnd 4: 1 inc, inserting the crochet hook simultaneously in the 1st st of rnd 3 and the 26th st of rnd 3, 11 sc, 1 inc (15 st).
Cut the yarn, keeping 10in (25cm) for sewing.

SMALL FINS X 2

In malachite green. Crochet in a spiral.
Rnd 1: 8 sc in a magic circle, well tightened (8 st).
Rnd 2: 7 inc, 1 sc, and 1 sl st in the same st (16 st).
Fold the round piece you just made in half.
Continue crocheting the two thicknesses simultaneously.
Rnd 3: 1 inc, inserting the crochet hook simultaneously in the 1st st of rnd 2 and in the 15th st of rnd 2, 5 sc, 1 inc (9 st).
Cut the yarn, keeping 10in (25cm) for sewing.

TAIL

In malachite green. In a magic circle, keeping 6in (15cm) of starting yarn, make: 1 sc, 1 hdc, 1 dc, 1 hdc, 1 sc.
Cut the yarn, keeping 6in (15cm) of yarn for sewing.

SHELL

Crochet in a spiral.
1st part
In malachite green.
Rnd 1: 6 sc in a magic circle (6 st).
Rnd 2: 6 inc (12 st).
Rnd 3: (1 sc, 1 inc) x 6 (18 st).
Rnd 4: (1 sc, 1 inc, 1 sc) x 6 (24 st).
Rnd 5: (1 inc, 3 sc) x 5, 1 inc, 2 sc, 1 sl st (30 st).
Stop the yarn invisibly.
2nd part
In water green.

Rnds 1 to 4: Repeat rnds 1 to 4 of the 1st part.
Rnd 5: (1 inc, 3 sc) x 6 (30 st).
Rnds 6 and 7: 30 st (30 st).
Position the 1st part of the shell back to back with the 2nd part. Crochet the next rnd by inserting the crochet hook simultaneously in both parts: Insert the crochet hook in both loops of the second part and in the BLO of the 1st part. Before making the last st, stuff the shell softly.
Rnd 8: 29 sc, 1 sl st (30 st).
Stop the yarn invisibly, then pull it into the shell several times before cutting it off flush with the surface.

ASSEMBLY

Each element must be sewn under the shell, where the two colors of green meet. Then bring each yarn to the inside, making several round trips in the body or the head, then cut it off flush with the surface.
Sew the head, making sure to place it the right way up so that the eyes are aligned when you look at them from the top. (If the head is placed upside down, the eyes seem offset.) Sew the last rnd of the head straddling 3 st of the underside of the shell.
Take a large and a small fin, and run the yarn to the inside so that it comes back out at the other end. All the fins will thus be facing the same direction once they are sewn.
Sew the two large fins 2 st away from the head, on each side, making sure to place the rounded part of the fins toward the front.
Sew the two small fins 5 st away from the large fins, making sure to place the rounded part of the fins toward the back.
Sew the tail between the two small fins.
With black Pearl Cotton, embroider a V-shaped smile between the eyes, over rnd 2.
If you wish, embroider or draw the cheeks according to the instructions given in the *Basic Shapes* section, p. 28.